THE
I HATE
MADONNA
HANDBOOK

THE
i hate
MADONNA
HANDBOOK

Ilene
Rosenzweig

St. Martin's Press/New York

Illustrations by Rick Geary

Grateful acknowledgment is made to the following for use of their photographs:

p. iii	Star File/Gene Shaw
P. ix	Star File
P. 2	Star File/Vinnie Zuffante
P. 19	Photofest/Andy Schwartz
P. 21	Top: AP/Wide World
	Bottom: AP/Wide World
P. 22	Photofest
P. 26	Photofest
P. 27	Photofest
P. 29	AP/Wide World
P. 31	Photofest
P. 32	AP/Wide World
P. 33	Star File/Vinnie Zuffante
P. 35	Star File/Gene Shaw
P. 36	Star File
P. 38	Star File/Bob Gruen
P. 39	Photofest
P. 42	AP/Wide World
P. 53	Star File
P. 54	Dan Gilroy
P. 54	Mark Kamins
P. 55	Top: Star File/Bob Gruen
	Bottom: Star File/Vinnie Zuffante
P. 56	Star File/Bill Warren
P. 56	Photofest
P. 57	Star File/Bob Scott
P. 58	Top: Star File/Vinnie Zuffante
	Bottom: Star File
P. 59	Bottom: Photofest
P. 60	Bottom: Star File/Gene Shaw
P. 61	Top: Star File
	Bottom: AP/Wide World
P. 62	Top: Star File/Vinnie Zuffante
	Bottom: Photofest
P. 64	Top: Photofest
	Bottom: Photofest
P. 65	Photofest
P. 67	Photofest
P. 68	Top: Photofest
	Bottom: Photofest
P. 69	Photofest
P. 71	Photofest
P. 72	Top: Photofest
	Bottom: Photofest
P. 73	Photofest
P. 74	Photofest
P. 75	Photofest
P. 80	Photofest
P. 81	Photofest
P. 82	AP/Wide World
P. 83	Top: Photofest
	Bottom: Photofest
P. 85	Top: Photofest
	Bottom: Photofest
P. 89	Star File/Brett Lee
P. 90	Star File/Vinnie Zuffante
P. 92	Star File/Vinnie Zuffante
P. 101	Star File
P. 111	Catherine McGann

Design by Jaye Zimet

Library of Congress Cataloging-in-Publication Data

Rosenzweig, Ilene.
    The I Hate Madonna Handbook / Ilene Rosenzweig.
    p. cm.
    ISBN 0-312-10480-4
    1. Madonna—Humor. 2. Rock music—Humor. I. Title.
    ML 420. M1387R67 1994
    782.42166.'092—dc20

93-44463
CIP
MN

First Edition: April 1994

10 9 8 7 6 5 4 3 2 1

This book is dedicated to two little girls, about four and six years old, who sat for hours one day, waiting in the lobby of the Westbury Hotel for their idol, Madonna. According to Madonna's personal assistant, Melinda Cooper, "We'd see them as we passed. Finally I said, 'They've been waiting here all day, Madonna. Why don't you sign an autograph for them?'" Madonna walked up to the little girls and said, "If I do it for you, then I'll have to do it for everybody. You're nothing. You don't mean anything to me." Then she turned and left.

Contents

Acknowledgments

With enormous thanks to Madonna's biographers, who have unearthed so much and must be credited with having far more patience for the ultimate Material subject than I could ever imagine: Mark Bego, *Madonna: Blonde Ambition* (Harmony Books, 1992); Christopher Anderson, *Madonna Unauthorized* (Island Books, published by Dell); Adam Sexton, *Desperately Seeking Madonna* (Delta Books, 1993); Norman King, *Madonna, The Book* (William Morrow, 1991); and Douglas Thompson, *Madonna Revealed* (Birch Lane Press, 1991). I am also indebted to the hundreds of daily reporters and paparazzi who have kept dutiful tabs on Madonna's every move for more than ten years, especially Richard Johnson, Linda Stasi, William Norwich, Frank DiGiaccomo, Cindy Adams, Charlotte Hayes, Suzy, Jeannie Williams, Lois Romano, George Rush, Page Six, "Inside New York," Liz Smith (even though she's a fan), and the editors and writers of *Vanity Fair* and *Rolling Stone* magazines who have provided in-depth reports on each Madonna phase with the unflagging precision of a German alarm clock.

Special thanks to the guys at Photofest, Michael Caruso, Reagan Arthur, Chris Calhoun, Debra Rosenzweig, P. U. Klein, Mike Santiago, Jeffrey Goldberg, Tim Warren, and, of course, Madonna, for her constant inspiration.

Introduction

This is a book for people who love to hate Madonna and for those who hate to love her. It's also a book for everyone who wonders when this woman will have had enough, start a perfume line, and call it quits.

Madonna would never be so polite. For more than ten years her cloud of hype has mushroomed, leaving no medium unscathed, no art form unsullied. And yet she keeps on ticking. Still bombing in the movie theaters, sucking the oxygen out of the airwaves, the dreaded Mega Star from Hell refuses to evaporate. What could she still possibly want?

"I want to rule the world," Madonna explains.

What a kidder.

The $100 million woman, one of the biggest, most powerful female entertainers in the world, is the leading guru of what culture critic Ron Rosenbaum describes as the "cult of the celebrity." With self-fueling star power, she has rocketed

ix

herself to a gravityless zone in the pop stratosphere. While the quality of her material has long been immaterial, she can rely on the masses to buy every belch. Madonna recites a fart poem and gets cheered by free-speech supporters. She unabashedly rips off the image of every style originator from Marilyn to Brando and is lauded as a marketing genius. She appears in a book of fantasies picturing herself hovering naked (but for a bunny-tail G-string) over a dog, or with a knife held to her vagina, and the pop culture Moonies delightedly cry: At last, a true feminist.

What's worse is she's inescapable. And, just when you think it's safe, when you shrug your shoulders and sigh, "Well, she's done it all," you turn around and . . . she's back. Again. Less and less like a virgin, more and more like Freddy Krueger with a 16-inch hard-on.

The I Hate Madonna Handbook is written not only for the staunch Madonna skeptics, but also for the disenchanted, those who unwittingly welcomed Madonna to the pop culture scene, who initially thought she was cute. In the beginning there didn't seem much to worry about. Just a small person with big armpits, whose songs were pre-chewed bubble gum and whose straining voice sounded as if it were emitted from an AM transistor radio. She seemed so desperate for attention. But then, in an MTV minute, the little girl with the bulge of baby fat above her Boy-Toy belt had turned into a one-woman army, with a Terminator body to boot. Before we knew what was happening, the pop urchin with the disheveled hair had traded her Salvation-Army-after-the-Hurricane wardrobe for an armor bra and a whip. Suddenly, Godzilla had seized control of our country and had started marching on the rest of the world.

Madonna grasped early on that what gives a star staying power is controversy. So she claimed to be political, claimed she had an agenda to "push people's buttons." But she later discovered that the voltage needed to be cranked ever higher to actually elicit a new shock. From the bouncy little number celebrating teenage pregnancy to the peep-show video where she kissed a 12-year-old boy on the mouth, her "politics" became more and more obtuse. By the time she trotted out the burning crosses in "Like a Prayer" and described on "Nightline" how bondage and the use of sadomasochistic paraphernalia in her "Justify My Love" video was supposed to be romantic and "loving," many who still wanted to like her just tuned out.

Madonna's popularity has cycloned out of control. Like zombies, people from Baton Rouge to Bangkok dress like her, hum her songs, and actually sit through her movies. Ivy League universities offer Madonna Studies courses, wherein students squander credits and hours deconstructing the lyrics to songs she claims to compose in fifteen minutes, drawing such conclusions as "Madonna decimates patriarchal and racist stereotypes simply in the way she utters 'self' in 'Express Yourself.'"

It is with reluctance that I have contributed to the already sagging shelves of Madonna-related product and literature, and engaged in the debate that always seems to lead to the conversation-stopping disclaimer: "Madonna, you've got to admit, is an amazing businesswoman, and she does show young women that it is possible to be sexual and powerful too." Please. Women have been making a killing with sexually seductive performances since Salome. The origin of the word *vamp* is vampire; the word *bombshell* explains itself. Sexually provocative women entertainers have long been stigmatized as dangerous destroyers, and Madonna, with her take-no-prisoners lingerie and boy-toy belligerence, fits neatly in the unfortunate tradition. The only difference is she runs her own shop. And in some parts of town, such a "businesswoman" is not heroicized as "the future of feminism," but is politely referred to as Madam.

Yet *The I Hate Madonna Handbook* is a hopeful book, perhaps a first step toward recovering from the tyranny of the Madonna Phenomenon: the success of style over substance and marketing skill over talent; the celebration of narcissism and of politics as phony as her hair color. Its pages offer a fun-filled tour of the Madonnamania that has reached epic proportions, unearthing head-shaking stories of her rise to fame and mind-numbing accounts of what a piece of work she is. By participating in its many fun and therapeutic anti-Madonna activities, you may just discover that Godzilla is really a housefly, and this book a swat that aims to put her ceaseless buzz to rest.

I

Desperately Seeking Stardom

Go-go boots, miniskirt, blonde hair, fake eyelashes—she was so cool!" In seventh grade, Madonna was just gaga about the fashion sense of her first rock idol, Nancy Sinatra. But what was even more appealing to the little go-go girl wannabe was the explicit bitchiness of Sinatra's number-one hit single, "These Boots Are Made for Walking." "That made one hell of an impression on me," Madonna recalled later. "When she said, 'Are you ready, boots, start walkin',' it was like, yeah, give me some of those go-go boots. I want to walk on a few people."

From that moment on, Madonna walked on A LOT of people—using them like steps on a StairMaster in her tireless climb toward the spotlight. "She's not an accident," Warren Beatty once said. But she's caused a few. Left like roadkill in her wake are trashed careers and emotional casualties: the managers, producers, friends, lovers, and family members who served their purpose and didn't get out of the way in time.

Below, a record of the well-meaning people who got too "close" to Madonna—and have the scars to prove it.

THE KEY TO HER SUCCESS

 WHITE GO-GO BOOTS
Degree stepped on.

 WHIP
Madonna used sex as an instrument of oppression.

 DOLLAR SIGN
She also cashed in on the victim's misfortune.

 TEARDROP
The victim suffered enduring pain or grief.

 SKIDMARKS
Collision left career on skids.

FIRST "SERIOUS" BOYFRIEND
Steve Bray

At the University of Michigan, Madonna dated Steve Bray, a drummer in a local R&B band. She was his moon-eyed groupie, tagging along to every gig in every HoJo and Holiday Inn that had a lounge and needed an act. Hanging around with Bray gave Madonna her first glimpse of how the music business worked. But after a year and a half, Madonna was ready to move on to the big time, so she quit college, bought a one-way ticket to New York, and left her "first love"—without even saying good-bye. "Looking back, I think I probably did make him feel kind of bad," she later admitted, "but I was really insensitive in those days. I was totally self-absorbed."

> "SOMETIMES I FEEL GUILTY BECAUSE I, LIKE, TRAVEL THROUGH PEOPLE. THAT'S TRUE OF A LOT OF AMBITIOUS PEOPLE. YOU TAKE WHAT YOU CAN AND THEN MOVE ON."—MADONNA

FIRST MANAGER
Camille Barbone

"Madonna says she's stepped on a lot of bodies to get where she is—I'm one of those bodies," says Camille Barbone, the manager who first discovered Madonna.

"One day there was a knock at my office door, and it was Madonna," Barbone has recalled. "She wanted me to listen to her tape....She needed money immediately. I gave her some. She wasn't shy about asking for more money after that....She seduced me psychologically. After that, I put her first, which was my downfall."

Madonna has admitted that during this period, when she was homeless, rummaging in garbage cans for scraps to eat, she "used to borrow money from people. . . . I'd let some poor sucker take me out to dinner and then I'd go, 'Can I borrow a hundred dollars?' I was always borrowing twenty-five, fifty, a hundred dollars from people."

Barbone brought the poor Material Girl into her spacious apartment on the Upper West Side, then when Madonna was able to find a studio apartment, it was Barbone who wrote the check. Barbone gave her a stipend of $100 a week and free run of her recording studio, Gotham Productions. In return, Madonna agreed to allow her Patron Saint to select her musicians, mold her act, and guide her career.

Barbone replaced the members of Madonna's fledgling band Emmy with top-notch studio musicians to back up Madonna. In an attempt to straighten out her protégée's priorities, Barbone also laid down several ground rules. Rule Number One: Madonna was not to sleep with any members of the revamped band. She promptly had an affair with the drummer, Bob Riley. Madonna admitted the affair and in the same breath told Barbone she wanted the unlucky drummer fired. It was around that time that Barbone realized Madonna was out of control. "I knew I had created a monster who would turn on me," she said later.

Madonna's ego started growing at an alarming rate. "I always want more. That's me. I'm a bitch and you're a bitch, but we work well together," she once told Barbone. Soon afterward, Madonna left her first manager.

FIRST BENEFACTORS
Jean Van Lieu

Jean Claude Pallerin

In early 1979, Van Lieu and Pallerin, two French producers who created disco sensation Patrick Hernandez ("Born to Be Alive"), plucked Madonna out of an audition for backup singers and dancers and offered to make her a star. "They promised me anything," Madonna has recounted. "They said, 'Come to Paris, we'll give you everything you want. You'll live like a queen, we'll give you a vocal coach, and you'll decide what direction you want to go in.' I did live like a queen and they did give me anything I wanted."

The producers whisked her from Charles de Gaulle Airport by limousine to an elegant Right Bank apartment, where in addition to her lavish accommodations and round-the-clock chauffuered limousine, her benefactors paid for a maid, a secretary, a vocal coach, and an unlimited wardrobe budget. Ricocheting from chic parties to dinners at Maxim's and Tour d'Argent, Madonna was toasted as the next Edith Piaf.

For any other unknown singer with a floundering career, this would have been a Cinderella fantasy come true. Not Madonna. She was incensed that the producers were also paying attention to Hernandez, their only other client. Madonna demanded that the producers give her the whole spotlight—despite the fact that she had not even cut a single and Hernandez was enjoying a worldwide hit.

She recalled how she suffered: "They dragged me to restaurants and no one would speak English to me."

According to Madonna, every time she griped, the producers gave her more money—and this somehow made her even madder.

"So once again I was playing the part of a rebel," she claimed. "I didn't want to do anything they wanted me to do. I gave my money away. I rode around on motorcycles all the time. I did everything I could to be bad. I kept saying, 'When are you going to do something with *me*?' And they were busy with Patrick."

Besides whining, a favorite pastime of Madonna and some of her biker friends was nearly sideswiping hapless American tourists, then yelling epithets at them in French. "I hung with Algerian and Vietnamese lowlifes who didn't have jobs but just drove around on motorcycles and terrorized people," she remembered.

By summer, Madonna was finally fed up with the favors of her two sugar daddies and had Van Lieu and Pallerin buy her a round-trip plane ticket—although she had no intention of keeping her word and returning. "I never signed a contract, so I wasn't obligated to stay there," she explained later.

The French producers, who had laid out thousands of dollars for Madonna, were shocked by her spectacular ingratitude. They may have been disappointed in themselves as well. After six months of coaching, their protégée hadn't even picked up the words most tourists learn their first day in France: *merci* and *au revoir*.

FIRST BANDMATE
Dan Gilroy

Back from Paris, Madonna, with nowhere else to go, landed on the doorstep of the boyfriend she had skipped out on six months before, Dan Gilroy. A nice Jewish boy who lived in an abandoned synagogue in Queens, Gilroy and his brother were putting together a band called Breakfast Club. For the better part of the next year, Gilroy not only provided Madonna with a basic musical education but also worked nine-to-five bussing tables in a local restaurant so that his fair-weather girlfriend could stay home and practice playing the drums.

When Madonna began campaigning to get into Breakfast Club, the Gilroys were skeptical. But Madonna wore them down, became Breakfast Club's drummer, and quickly seized control of the band. "I was just a lot more goal-oriented and commercial-minded than they were," Madonna explained. "I wanted to know everything they knew, because I knew I could make it work to my benefit....It was one of the happiest times of my life."

Before long, however, Madonna was unhappy again. Her flailing drumsticks, it seems, were no match for the band's star attraction, a sultry bass player with natural blonde hair named Angie Smit. Upstaged, Madonna pushed the Gilroy brothers to kick her competition out of the band, which they finally did.

Soon after, having, in her own words, "sucked what I needed" from Gilroy and his brother, Madonna announced that the affair was over and that she was moving back to Manhattan to start her own band.

THE FIRST PRODUCERS
Steve Bray

Mark Kamins

Reggie Lucas

When Madonna was putting together her own band, one of her first phone calls was to her old Michigan boyfriend Steve Bray. Madonna wanted Bray to take musical control of the band. She recognized that she wasn't an experienced enough musician to do the job.

Lured by the prospect of a profitable collaboration with Madonna's first band, Bray left for New York the following week. For the next couple of years, he lived the life of a struggling musician with Madonna, sleeping in rehearsal studios and eating meals of yogurt and peanuts. All his money was spent to record demo tapes of four songs they had cowritten: "Everybody," "Burning Up," "Stay," and "Ain't No Big Deal."

> "ALL MY BOYFRIENDS HAVE TURNED OUT TO BE VERY HELPFUL TO MY CAREER, EVEN IF THAT'S NOT THE ONLY REASON I STAYED WITH THEM."
> —MADONNA

Madonna's first big break came from Mark Kamins, the popular deejay at the Danceteria nightclub. She persuaded him to play the tape of "Everybody" with her tried-and-true technique. "I was flirting with him," she explained later. Kamins offered her a deal: If he could get her a record contract, he would be the producer of her first album. She agreed enthusiastically—neglecting to mention that she had already promised the job to her boyfriend Bray.

Kamins used his contact with Seymour Stein, president of Sire Records, to get Madonna signed. "Seymour believed in me," recalled Kamins. "So he said, 'Okay, give it a shot.'" Kamins began by producing Madonna's first single, "Everybody," which shot up to number three on the dance charts.

Once it was time to cut the album, Madonna broke the news to Bray that he wouldn't be the producer; as a consolation prize, she offered him the job of musical arranger. "Fuck you," he replied succinctly. "Either I produce or nothing." And nothing it was. Bray, enraged over what he believed to be yet another betrayal by Madonna, refused to speak to her for nearly two years.

Madonna then topped herself by bouncing Kamins in favor of a better-connected producer named Reggie Lucas, who she hired to produce the album. "Yes, I was hurt, and very pissed off!" Kamins said afterward. "She wanted someone who was better on vocals and she was right. That's not my forte. But it was the way it was handled. Madonna never told me to my face that I was replaced by Reggie Lucas. I had to find out from the guys at Warner." Madonna did sign a document giving Kamins a percentage of the royalties. Kamins later became embroiled in a cumbersome legal battle with Madonna to enforce the agreement and finally settled out of court.

The first album, *Madonna*, was surprisingly successful. Lucas "is a good producer," Madonna said at the time, "very open and sensitive." So when it came time to record the follow-up, Lucas naturally expected to be rewarded for his hard work. But Madonna, not missing a beat, hip-checked Lucas to the side for an even more powerful producer, Nile Rodgers.

MUSICAL RIVAL
Manny Parrish

In early 1984, Italian clothing designer Elio Fiorucci put Madonna on the bill at Studio 54 for the birthday party of his store. She was scheduled to go on at 2 A.M., after a two-hour set by Manny Parrish. "She was on a fucking rampage—as usual," Parrish later recalled. She wanted to go on at midnight when the room was full, not later on. [But] I was the headliner, so to speak, and she wasn't."

First, according to Parrish, "She told us that I wasn't going on at midnight, that she was, and that things were switched around. So everybody left the room and started walking around the club. She did this to fuck up my act, and the stage manager came in and said, 'Hey, you're going on in twenty minutes—where is everybody? What's going on?' I told him, 'Well, Madonna said we're going on second, and she's going on first.' And he said, 'WHAT?!?' and ran into her room and started screaming at her."

But Madonna wasn't finished. "That fucking bitch stole my fucking jackets!" reported Parrish. "We had our costumes—we had graffiti jackets from Kansai, and we were getting ready to go on—and they were missing! So, we're looking around, and looking around, and looking around, and one of her dancers came in from outside, and said, 'Look, she'll kill me if she finds me in here, but your costumes are hidden behind the boiler—in the back over there.' Somebody hid them, and her dancer was implying that it was her. And they were plastic, so I had to soak them in ice water to keep them from melting!"

FASHION DESIGNER
Maripol

Madonna's first trademark style, the punky junky ragbag look that made her a recognizable commodity, included the dozens of rubber bracelets—actually O-rings used as drive belts on typewriters—that were found by a jewelry designer named Maripol.

Maripol designed Madonna's costume for the MTV Awards and for the cover of her second album, *Like a Virgin*. But Maripol was more than just an accessory designer. She was also a well-connected French socialite, introducing Madonna to the likes of Mick Jagger, Andy Warhol, and Debbie Harry, and she soon became Madonna's confidante and surrogate mother. "Maripol would tell Madonna not to waste her time with people who were no longer on top," said Madonna's friend Erica Bell. "Power and influence were the name of the game. If a person couldn't do Madonna's career any good, she ignored them. Madonna could be very brutal that way."

Sometimes even socialites have to earn a living, and when

Madonna signed a huge merchandizing deal with a big clothing company, Maripol made plans to supply her "Lucky Star" jewelry to the stores that were stocking the official Boy Toy fashions. In the summer of 1986, however, Madonna changed her look—without warning her old friend. "Maripol had it made until Madonna instantly changed her image," said a friend of Maripol's. "In her loft on Broadway, Maripol still has cases and cases of 'Lucky Star' jewelry she thought she was going to market—stars and rubber crosses. Madonna simply took off ahead of Maripol, and basically said, 'Hey, tough!'" Maripol's company went bankrupt soon afterward.

YOUNG PROTÉGÉE
Cheyne

Nearing the final cut of *Desperately Seeking Susan*, director Susan Seidelman asked Madonna if she had a song she could use in the film to boost its box-office potential. Madonna brought in a tape of "Into the Groove," which the director loved. But Madonna had already promised the song to an up-and-coming black singer named Cheyne, who had recently recorded a version for her own debut album. So Madonna found herself in a dilemma: whether to keep her word or promote herself. Coincidentally, Cheyne's producer was Mark Kamins, the Danceteria deejay Madonna had dumped as the producer of her first album. Faced with the possibilty of shafting Cheyne, as well as Kamins for a second time, Madonna could not resist the temptation to promote herself. "Cheyne saw that Madonna was doing 'Into the Groove' and she freaked," recalled Kamins. "Cheyne screamed, 'I won't be the black Madonna!' It was a betrayal of Cheyne, and as a young singer trying to make it, she was devastated, but Madonna couldn't have cared less."

CHOREOGRAPHER AND PERSONAL FRIEND
Karole Armitage

In early 1990, Madonna hired her friend Karole Armitage to choreograph the *Blonde Ambition* concert tour. Armitage relocated from New York to Los Angeles and cast all the dancers before Madonna whimsically changed her mind and replaced Armitage with another choreographer. Armitage reported that Madonna had been upset at the choreographer's independent ideas. "Hire and fire, hire and fire" was how Madonna described her mantra during the seven months it took to assemble a staff for the tour.

FAMILY MEMBERS
Martin

Dad

Mom

Christopher

Madonna's family members may not have been able to help her during her rise to the top, but they did provide some real-life material for her backstage movie, *Truth or Dare.*

   • Madonna's brother Martin is shown, just out of an alcohol

rehab clinic, pathetically trying to pick up one of the backup singers. "My brother's crazy," Madonna warns her bodyguards with a smirk. Then, after a performance, he fails to turn up for a visit at her hotel. When he shows up the next night too late, she refuses to let him in.

• Madonna's devoutly Catholic father also serves as fodder in the film. In one scene, Madonna tells Sandra Bernhard about a night during her childhood when she was afraid to sleep alone and crawled into her father's bed. "I went right to sleep," says Madonna. "After he fucked me. Just kidding!" Ha ha.

• Madonna even digs up the memory of her mother, who passed away three decades ago, when she films her first visit to the gravesite since childhood. Lolling about on her mother's grave, Madonna wonders about "what she looks like now. Just a bunch of dust."

Madonna outed her younger brother Christopher in an interview with *Advocate* magazine. In what appears to have been an effort to establish her credentials in the gay community, Madonna cited her special relationship with Christopher: "My brother Christoper's gay, and he and I have always been the closest members of my family." She said she first realized Christopher was gay when she brought him to ballet class and he met her gay dance teacher. "I just saw something between them," she said. "I can't even tell you exactly what. But then I thought, 'Oh, I get it. Oh, okay. He likes men, too.' It was this incredible revelation."

Sharing her "incredible revelation," Madonna exposed her younger brother's sexuality to the scrutiny of the world. Christopher was rocked by the disclosure, partly because it forced their father to confront his son's homosexuality. According to *Advocate* editor Richard Rouilard, "Her brother was very upset—it had not been carefully discussed with him, and he asked us to edit out that part of the interview." But by that time the magazine had already gone to press and Christopher was left to cope with the consequences of his sister's thoughtlessness.

PSEUDO-FAMILY MEMBERS

Oliver Crumes

Kevin A. Stea

Gabriel Trupin

In *Truth or Dare*, Madonna often referred to the dancers from the *Blonde Ambition* tour as "my children" and made such caring gestures as supplying condoms in their per diem expense envelopes. "Madonna said she would do anything for us," recalled one dancer, Kevin A. Stea, "that she would give us the shirt off her back." Soon after the movie's release, however, three of her kids filed a lawsuit against her, her company, and film distributor Miramax Films. Stea, Oliver Crumes, and Gabriel Trupin accused Madonna of "invasion of privacy, fraud, deceit, intentional misrepresentation, suppression of fact, and intentional infliction of emotional distress." The suit is still awaiting trial.

When it became clear that Madonna had a bigger picture in mind than gathering footage for "private home movies for personal use," the dancers expressed concern. They were allegedly reassured that they would be allowed to review the final product and edit out any scenes they found objectionable. But when Trupin saw a scene that showed him kissing another male dancer on a dare from Madonna, he was horrified. Despite Madonna's claims to the contrary, Trupin says that he never signed a release. With his family unaware of his sexual orientation, Trupin implored Madonna to cut the footage. In response, Madonna flew into a rage. "Get over it!" she screamed. "I don't care!" The scene remained in the film.

2
The Madonna Hall of Shamelessness

21 Lowlights in a Career of Amazing Disgrace

Welcome to Madonna's Hall of Shamelessness, the museum dedicated to the classic works of exhibitionism, self-promotion, and hypocrisy by Our Lady of Perpetual Hype. Please excuse the scaffolding. We're in the process of expansion, as always.

Today we will be touring the permanent collection, entitled "I'm Not Ashamed of Anything." The exhibit, which features the best of Madonna at her worst, spans her life from her stage debut in 1969, when she performed as a go-go dancer in elementary school, to her cataclysmic arrival as the World's Most Overexposed Flasher.

There will be moments on the tour when you will feel yourself blushing and wanting to avert your eyes. Go ahead. This is a normal response in our interactive museum-going experience. You are now ready to proceed to the next panel. If you do not have these reactions, however, you may want to consult a therapist. You may be suffering from symptoms of psychopathy, the absence of shame, or guilt. Or you may be Madonna.

1969

It was standing room only at St. Andrew's School the night of the annual talent show, an exciting moment in a hardworking neighborhood near Detroit. The parish faithful were getting the snapshots they had come for: cute kids in tap shoes, poetry from short angels.

Then out came Madonna Louise Veronica Ciccone.

Every eyeball froze. People looked as if they'd been slapped, and somewhere in the crowd, the molecules of her father's face rearranged themselves into granite. There he sat—a by-the-book, God-fearing man—watching his fifth-grade daughter dance in the nude.

That's how it looked at first. "I was practically naked," Madonna has recalled, still laughing at the memory. "But the talent show was my one night a year to show them who I really was and what I could really be. And I just wanted to do totally outrageous stuff."

So she wore a next-to-nothing bikini and coated herself top to bottom in swirls of fluorescent green paint—"sort of a flower-power thing"—that shimmered in the lights. Up came hard-rock music and on went Madonna, undulating wildly around the stage. It was 1969 and Madonna was doing her rendition of Goldie Hawn go-going on "Laugh-In," a typical Madonna performance—part talent, part rip-off, part joke, part sex. And the crowd loved it. At least that's how Madonna remembers that remarkable night, and she won, of course. "And boys chased me after that, but no girls would talk to me and my father grounded me for two weeks. Oh, he was so horrified. 'How could you do that to me?' he said." Poor man. He didn't know then that it was just the beginning.

As reported by Richard Price, *USA Weekend*, June 10, 1990

September 14, 1984

At the first annual MTV Video Music Awards, Madonna crawls onstage in a white wedding dress and simulates masturbation in front of millions of viewers in the first public performance of "Like a Virgin."

March 29, 1985

The film *Desperately Seeking Susan* is released. Madonna's feature-film debut is enthusiastically received by reviewers and audiences. She steals the show with a role that fits her like a fingerless glove: a gum-snapping vagabond who might have crawled out of a thrift shop explosion. Madonna would never again reach the acting heights she attained in *Desperately*. Some critics, puzzling over the mystery of Madonna's anomolous success in the role of Susan, have wagered that Madonna is not acting in the movie at all, that the only character she portrays in the film is her own.

Director Susan Seidelman declared that "there is a lot of Madonna in Susan." Madonna herself said: "I thought I shared a lot with [my character]....She's a clever con artist and she doesn't let you know when you're being conned."

Was Madonna acting...or just acting like herself?

17

SUSAN

...wakes up in a strange man's hotel room and takes a Polaroid picture of herself.

MADONNA

...quits the acting lessons Camille Barbone had enrolled her in after one day, preferring to stretch out on the floor of her living room and take Polaroids of herself. (Madonna complained that the acting coach, the renowned Mira Rostova, was "mean" and the lessons were "too hard." Rostova gave a failing grade to her one-day pupil: "This girl will never be an actress," she told Barbone. "She is too vulgar, and she thinks she knows it all. Besides, I do not like her.")

SUSAN

...vandalizes lockers at the Port Authority bus terminal with a nail file.

MADONNA

...vandalizes the limousine sent by Warner Brothers Records to pick her up at the airport in Paris before a fashion party by scrawling "Boy Toy" in indelible marker across the upholstery.

SUSAN

...gets arrested for stiffing a taxi-cab driver.

MADONNA

...shows up at her audition for the role of Susan in a cab she couldn't pay for. "So here she is," recalled director Susan Seidelman, "meeting with a bunch of movie people for a job and the first thing she does is hit us up for cab fare. It was exactly what Susan would have done!"

SUSAN

...tries to shoplift a pair of shoes she admires in the store window.

MADONNA

...goes on shoplifting sprees at Mitzelfeld's Department Store and D&C Dime Store in Rochester, Michigan, while she is in high school. Friends remember that she always got away with more stolen merchandise than anyone else.

SUSAN

...plays sex games with her boyfriend on a pinball machine in a bar.

MADONNA

...is pictured playing sex games with a boyfriend on a pinball machine in a bar in *Sex*.

THE NAVEL BATTLE. In this historic week, Madonna bares all to the American public in not one but two pornographic magazines, and makes her grandmother cry.

On July 7, *Penthouse* magazine declares that it will publish sixteen pages of photos of Madonna nude, taken in 1979-80 during her career as an artist's model. The battle of the girlie magazines begins the following day, as *Playboy* announces it will bumrush *Penthouse* to the newsstands by publishing their own collection of snapshots of naked Madonna first. *Penthouse* publisher Bob Guccione is stunned to see Madonna nudes suddenly surfacing like German U-boats. "They came from many different sources," he said. "Photography teachers, their students, amateurs, professionals." Still reeling from the *Playboy* bombshell, Guccione concedes that his Madonna pics were, well, less than buff: "She wasn't well groomed, there was lots of hair on her arms and hair sticking out of her armpits." Guccione offers Madonna $1 million to pose with the photographer of her choice in a vain effort to get a set of Madonna nudes that would be up to the porno mag's usual standards. Madonna declines. When Guccione realizes that the Madonna Navel War is not a contest of quality but of speed, he dashes to the kiosks with his September issue on July 11, only to discover that *Playboy* has arrived first, just hours before.

Meanwhile, on the West Coast, the Pop Pin-Up was not amused. Having signed releases for her standard $25 modeling fees, she had relinquished control to the photographers. Helpless to prevent the publication of the nudes, or to make more money from them, she resorted to her all-purpose battle cry. "I'm not ashamed of anything!" she said through spokesperson Liz Rosenberg, neglecting to mention her failed efforts to sue the two magazines in an attempt to keep the nudes out of circulation.

Some Madonna intimates did not recover so quickly. Back in

Bay City, Michigan, Elsie Fortin found out about her granddaughter's skin mag debut when she was watching "Donahue." "I was shocked," Grandma Fortin said later. "I was all alone and I started to cry."

August 2, 1985

Videocassettes of Madonna's first movie, *A Certain Sacrifice*, go on sale across the country. Madonna stars as Bruna, a denizen of the Lower East Side who simulates fellatio with a gas pump and has an orgy with a "family of lovers"—a man, a woman, and a drag queen—in which she bares her breasts and has multiple orgasms. After Bruna professes her love for the film's protagonist, but explains that she can't leave her group-sex partners, she is brutally raped in a diner bathroom by a character named Raymond Hall. To avenge the crime, Bruna enlists the aid of her sex slaves, who hunt down and kidnap the rapist, and then execute him on the Brooklyn Bridge. The scene turns into a musical number as the family of lovers dismember the rapist and drink his blood, while singing "Raymond Hall Must Die Today."

Unlike other actors who have worked in porno movies during their lean years because they were desperate for money, Madonna performed in this "midnight movie" on a gratis basis, just for the—ahem—exposure.

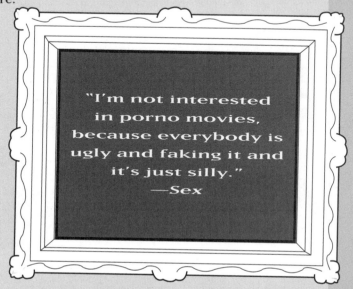

"I'm not interested in porno movies, because everybody is ugly and faking it and it's just silly."
—*Sex*

22

January 1986

Filming begins on *Shanghai Surprise*, Madonna's first film with hubbie Sean Penn. The newlywed couple arrived in Macao, on mainland China, with lovelights in their eyes, but their honeymoon collaboration was quickly spoiled by the difficulties of making a movie behind the bamboo curtain. The result was an indigestible mess in which Madonna is cast in the unlikely role of a prim missionary and Sean plays a tie salesman mixed up in opium smuggling.

More memorable than the movie itself was the outrageous behavior that would earn the couple the nickname "the Poison Penns" and a worldwide reputation as "the most offensive people on the planet," as the New York *Daily News* put it. Below, a Pu Pu Platter of Poison Penn dish:

SIZZLING BEEF

Sean's bodyguards "punch out" 61-year-old Leonel Borralho, owner of two newspapers in Macao when he tries to photograph the twosome in the Oriental Hotel. Penn's bodyguards refuse to let Borralho leave until he turns over the film, which he does in exchange for the promise of an exclusive interview. When the Penns fail to honor the promise, Borralho files assault charges and sues for damages of $1 million. Madonna responds by calling Borralho "a jerk" and lashes out at her fans as people who "lead such boring lives" that fantasizing about stars is their only escape.

SPIT AND RUN

When the Penns arrive in London to finish shooting, Madonna's limousine accidentally runs over a photographer's foot. Sean expresses his remorse later that day when he spits in the face of another photographer.

WHILE MY GUITAR GENTLY WEEPS

Madonna consents to a press conference in London. Asked if she is a Beatles fan, Madonna, who is seated next to George Harrison, the film's producer, cracks: "I was too young for Beatlemania." When a reporter inquires what she thinks of England, the ambassador of American good will replies, "It must be lovely, somewhere." Asked how she feels about the run-ins and run-overs with English journalists and commoners, she says with a shrug: "I have nothing to apologize for."

WORD OF MOUTH

Adding insult to injury, the Penns don't just ignore *Shanghai Surprise*, they bad-mouth it. "The director turned out not to know what he was doing," says Madonna. "We were on a ship without a captain.... [I]f it was directed poorly, you can't imagine how poorly it was edited. "They were the essence of non-cooperation," says Greg

Morrison, president of marketing for MGM, the film's distributor. "They had done nothing, absolutely nothing, to help sell the film. Stars like Marlon Brando and Frank Sinatra never had the greatest relationship with the press, but you had to bow to Sinatra's singing, to Brando's acting. What you've got today is a lot of young people like Sean and Madonna with fictional star power, who are basking in celebrityhood that's not translating into ticket sales."

I WANT MY MTV

Released over Labor Day weekend in the parts of the country where Madonna's records sell best, the movie opens to empty houses. George Harrison implores Madonna to do a video to support the movie, but she turns him down flat. After having defended her to the press throughout the turbulent course of the film, Harrison is angry and hurt that Madonna has turned her back on him and his investment. He finally concedes, "The press was right about her."

BOX OFFICE POISON

Shanghai Surprise, which cost Harrison $17 million to make, grosses a deplorable $2.2 million.

January 1988

Madonna films her role as Hortense Hathaway, a good-hearted showgirl, in *Bloodhounds of Broadway*, a Roaring Twenties comedy based on short stories by Damon Runyon. The movie is destined to be such a stinker that it can't be released and goes directly to the "Videos From Hell" section at rental stores. Matt Dillon, Jennifer Grey, Randy Quaid, and the rest of the ensemble cast have little to be proud of—but at least they try to hold on to their dignity. Madonna, however, is stripped of hers at her own behest. Between takes, Madonna complains to the wardrobe mistress that her dress is uncomfortable. Told to take the costume off to be refitted, she promptly rips it off in front of everyone on the set. Her only underwear is a garter belt.

August 6, 1987

Ten thousand fans mob Times Square for the premiere of *Who's That Girl?* Madonna pulls up in her limo an hour late, then steps up onto a platform on a traffic island and addresses her cheering, patiently waiting fans: "Shut up so I can talk!"

They do. But after the screening they must have started talking again. The next day, not even the most devoted fans turn out to see Madonna in this splashing belly flop. At its first regularly scheduled performance, at Manhattan's 1,151-seat Ziegfeld Theater, sixty people are in the house. The $20 million movie grosses an anemic $5.1 million in its first nine days before plummeting to a mercifully quick death. *Who's That Girl?* does manage one noteworthy achievement: It went from big screen to video in a record three months.

December 1986

The "Open Your Heart" video is released. Surrounded by a Felliniesque assortment of voyeurs leering at her from windowed booths, the bustier-clad Madonna struts and prances as the writhing star of a sleazy peep show. The video ends with her kissing a 12-year-old boy full on the mouth, then happily skipping off with him into the night.

Madonna intends this "tiny classic" to ignite another debate over decency, which it does—in her house. Sean Penn fumes over the video, in which his wife portrays every pervert's fantasy, and he is, in the words of one friend, "sickened" by the sight of her lasciviously kissing a child. One of their famous door-slamming, name-calling rows ensues and Madonna again flees to New York. She spends the holiday season being comforted by her reported lover, model Nick Kamen.

March 2, 1989

Madonna signs to do her first-ever endorsement for an American product, Pespi-Cola. She is untroubled by any accusation of selling out. "I like the challenge of merging art and commerce," she says. "As far as I'm concerned, making a video is also a commercial."

They seem like a perfect match: Pepsi, the company that made a $44 billion consumer product of colored sugar water, and Madonna, the self-marketeer who created a $100 million consumer product of

105 pounds of hot air and hair coloring. The global spot, produced by the BBDO advertising firm, is the biggest purchase of TV time ever made and will debut Madonna's title song from her new album, *Like a Prayer*, which Pepsi was hoping would become the drink's new marketing anthem.

Then the shit hits the can.

"One day," remembers BBDO executive Roger Mosconi,

"Madonna, who likes to joke with me, came up to me and said, 'Hey, Roger, are you going to have the burning crosses reflecting in the Pepsi can?' And I said, 'What burning crosses?' And she smiled and teased, 'You'll see.'"

Madonna keeps executives at BBDO in the dark about the controversial nature of the independently produced video that she has already shot for "Like a Prayer"—despite the fact that they were paying her $5 million for her endorsement. In the video, Madonna sees a black man arrested for a crime he didn't commit, then goes to church, where she makes sure to remove her robe before praying to a black saint who looks just like the unjustly accused man. An unintelligible series of flashbacks and fantasies follows, including: Madonna falling through the sky into the arms of a pretty black choir singer; Madonna inflicting herself with stigmata wounds; Madonna boogying down with the pretty choir singer and the rest of the good-time gospel. Scenes of Madonna dancing in her slip before a field of burning crosses are intercut with those of her making love to the saint/accused man in the church.

When the heretical video is released, Pepsi is bowled over by the backlash. The American Family Association labels it blatantly offensive and orders a one-year nationwide boycott of all Pepsi products. The Roman Catholic bishop of Corpus Christi, Texas, joins the boycott. "Obviously I'm tapping into something in their subconscious that they're very ashamed of..." Madonna muses nonsensically. "It's like Hitler—they want to purify your thoughts."

Pepsi is ultimately forced to cancel the campaign entirely, costing the company millions. Only Madonna could make a multi-billion-dollar conglomerate into an innocent victim. "She wanted there to be a big splash," a Madonna ex-staffer says, adding that she was actually pleased when Pepsi was forced to yank their ad. "That way she got the headlines she felt she needed to sell the album, and she got to keep the five million dollars, too."

June 30, 1986

Madonna releases the video for "Papa Don't Preach," endearing herself to conservatives who praise what they describe as its positive pro-life message. Even Tipper Gore, leader of the censorious Parents Music Resource Center, applauds. The video is a romping minidrama of a tough street kid (Madonna) who eyes a hunky guy on a Staten Island street corner, and instantly becomes pregnant with his child. Undisturbed by the prospect of being pregnant, and the fact that the baby's father doesn't seem to be making any commitment, Madonna only worries that her father will disapprove. Luckily, all her troubles melt away when Dad (Danny Aiello) wrestles with the news for less than a video minute before giving Madonna an accepting hug.

But it turns out that Madonna didn't practice what she preached! "I wish that I was married and in a situation where having a child would be possible," she said later to *Vanity Fair*. "People say, 'Well, have one on your own.' I say, 'Wait a minute, I'm not interested in raising a cripple.' I want a father there. I want someone I can depend on."

Madonna's hypocrisy doesn't stop there. According to sources close to Madonna, by the time she made the "Papa Don't Preach" video she had had several abortions herself. On the eve of her first American tour, recalled Melinda Cooper, assistant to Madonna's longtime manager Freddy DeMann, "Madonna was pregnant with Jellybean [Benitez]'s baby....So we arranged for Madonna to have the abortion, drove her to the doctor's office, everything. She seemed so innocent at the time; it wasn't until much later that I learned she had had others. But Madonna wasn't about to let something like a baby interfere with the tour." Erica Bell, an old friend, has confirmed that "Madonna had several abortions when she was with Jellybean—at least three that I know of."

June 18, 1988

In the middle of a Broadway performance of David Mamet's *Speed-the-Plow*, Madonna is reading from a book about radiation and the end of the world when she suddenly bursts out laughing. She is supposed to be telling the studio chief, played by Joe Mantegna, that the book would make a good movie. Instead, she giggles for several minutes as the Royale Theatre audience buzzes uncomfortably and Mantegna tries to maintain his composure. Hissing is heard in the balcony. Finally regaining control, she resumes with "I was saying..." and the scripted dialogue.

The breach of character is the main topic of conversation during intermission and after the second act. "The laughter certainly isn't in the script," admits the play's spokesman.

We can only guess what it was about radiation that caused Madonna's fit of giggles, but perhaps her evaluation of Mamet's play sheds a little light on her lapse. "It was a real mind-fuck of a script," she would later say. "Brilliant but confusing."

May 24, 1989

At the "Bungle the Jungle" concert, a benefit planned to raise money for the preservation of the tropical rain forests, Madonna and Sandra Bernhard sing a raunchy rendition of Sonny and Cher's "I Got You Babe." Wearing matching graffiti-splashed jeans and sequined bras, the couple grab their crotches, rub against each other, and generally simulate sex. The audience is appalled. Bernhard grabs Madonna from behind, thrusts her pelvis suggestively, and sways to the beat. Madonna tells the crowd, "Don't believe those stories!" referring to the rumors circulating at the time that the two were lesbian lovers. Bernhard counters, "Believe those stories!"

Bernhard later acts indignant as she explains their behavior: "The way we act together is a political statement....The rain forest is dying. What do you care more about, the rain forest or our sexuality?"

One might ask her the same question.

33

December 3, 1990

Madonna appears on ABC News "Nightline" to defend her "Justify My Love" video, which has been rejected by MTV for its overt sexual and sadomasochistic content.

The week before, Madonna claimed the video merely showed "the interior of a human being's mind. These fantasies and thoughts exist in every person," she said, adding that the video is "romantic and loving." The romantic and loving images we apparently all carry around with us include: Madonna in a bedroom forcing her lover to watch her have sex with another man who wears too much eye shadow; Madonna having her lover chained to a chair while a dominatrix fondles him menacingly; Madonna having sex with her lover in front of an audience of gay men in freaky makeup, lesbians in black leather, and a demonic man who dances around in a cat suit.

Supposedly distressed about the controversy she has stirred up, Madonna makes an unlikely appearance on the cerebral ABC News show "Nightline." Ted Koppel has wisely chosen to take the night off, however, and the show is hosted by Forrest Sawyer. Below, an adapted excerpt from the Auteur's attempt to Justify Her Video.

Forrest Sawyer: First you have to tell me where you draw the line [on censorship].

Madonna: Well, okay, I draw the line in terms of what I think is viewable on television. I draw the line where . . . with violence and humiliation and degradation, okay? And I don't think any of these issues are evident in my video. That's where I draw the line. That's what I don't want to see, you know?

Forrest Sawyer: Then I guess that one woman's art is another woman's pornography. I'm thinking of the "Express Yourself" video.

Madonna: Mmm-hmm.

Forrest Sawyer: I mean, there are images of you chained. There are images of you crawling under a table.

Madonna: Yes, but I am chained—

Forrest Sawyer: And there are a lot of people upset by that.

Madonna: Yes, yes. Okay, I've chained myself, though, okay? No—there wasn't a man that put that chain on me. I did it myself. I was chained to my desires. I crawled under my own table, you know? There wasn't a man standing there making me do it. I do everything by my own volition. I'm in charge, okay? Degradation is when somebody else is making you do something against your wishes, okay?... I put myself in these situations with men, you know, and everybody knows, you know, in terms of my image in the public, people don't think of me as a person who's not in charge of my career or my life, okay? And isn't that what feminism is all about, you know, equality for men and women? And aren't I in charge of my life, doing the things I want to do? Making my own decisions?

May 13, 1991

Madonna makes a grand entrance at the forty-fourth annual Cannes Film Festival before the screening of her combination autodocumentary/publicity orgy *Truth or Dare*. Though the film is not eligible for any awards at the festival, Madonna hangs around in Cannes for more than a week, determined to have her way with the press by—what else—taking off her clothes in public.

At the premiere of *Truth or Dare*, Madonna emerges from a white limousine wearing a conspicuous pink kimono. She traipses up the steps of the Palais du Festival and does a Marilyn Monroe turn to the assembled cameras; flinging open her Madame Butterfly cape, she offers them a leer at her white satin bra and girdle.

"I didn't know she was going to do that," says Miramax Films' Harvey Weinstein, who was in Madonna's entourage that night. "When she showed them her underwear or whatever that was, the barricades came down and the screening was over."

"What did you attempt to show?" a French TV interviewer later asks. "The truth," Madonna replies.

May 1991

In *Truth or Dare*, the backstage chronicle of her *Blonde Ambition* tour, director Alek Keshishian captured the fun-loving, vulnerable, nurturing mother figure Madonna considers herself to be. She describes the filming process as a journey of self-discovery. Not surprisingly she likes what she found. She tells *Rolling Stone*, "I learned to love myself. Everybody should make documentaries about themselves."

What inspired her self-love? Well, writhing around on her mother's grave, simulating oral sex with an Evian water bottle, reciting a fart poem, ordering one of her dancers to expose himself, describing sexual games with childhood friend Moira McFarland before coldly dismissing the woman as she begs Madonna to be the godmother of her child. Perhaps her most lovable moment comes when she finds out that her shy, overweight young makeup woman has been sexually assaulted during the tour, waking up in her hotel room naked and bleeding. In response, Madonna giggles as she comments, "She must have told someone she was on the tour and they wanted to fuck with her."

November 13, 1991

A doll of Madonna's Breathless Mahoney character in *Dick Tracy* makes the annual list of "10 Worst Toys." Edward M. Swartz, the author of the consumer safety books *Toys That Kill* and *Toys That Don't Care*, says the removable vinyl arms of the 10-inch doll modeled after Madonna pose a choking hazard to young Madonna fans.

October 15, 1992

Madonna celebrates the publication of her first literary effort, *Sex,* a collection of fantasies, poetry, and photos. While most of America gathers around their television sets to watch the final presidential debate between incumbent George Bush, third-party candidate Ross Perot, and future President Bill Clinton, Madonna hosts a party at Industria, a party space in Manhattan. The goings-on include: two men in black leather hanging on chains hooked to the ceiling; a naked woman sitting in a bathtub filled with popcorn that guests can paw through; a female bathroom attendant crouching on all fours and being whipped with a cat-o'-nine tails; a woman in army boots wrapping another woman in electrical tape; a blonde post-operative transsexual dressed in fishnet stockings and a hat working at a kissing booth; couples simulating sex on mounted platforms; a man having Madonna's face tattooed on his buttock, a sight which Madonna, wearing a "Heidi from Hell" outfit complete with coiled braids and a stuffed toy lamb, acknowledges approvingly. "I'm honored," she says. Upstairs, the presidential debate plays on a small TV that no one watches.

January 1993

This month marks the release of *Body of Evidence*, a movie in which Madonna plays a psychotic nymphomaniac who murders her rich elderly lover with rough sex. She then seduces her married trial lawyer (Willem Dafoe), introducing him to the joys of S&M by dripping hot candle wax on his genitals, and making love on top of a car covered with shattered glass. At a test screening of the movie, the audience laughs and boos at dialogue like this:

Madonna: Have you ever seen animals make love, Frank? It's intense. It's violent. But they never hurt each other.
Frank: We're not animals.
Madonna: Yes, we are.

Cheers are heard only once: when Madonna is slapped in the face by Dafoe's screen wife.

Madonna ends her performance as musical guest on "Saturday Night Live" by tearing up a photo of Joey Buttafuoco, the Long Island car mechanic whose underage lover, Amy Fisher, shot his wife in the head. Then Madonna beckoned all to "Fight the real enemy!"

Fisher might have missed her mark, but when Madonna shoots she scores! In one deft gesture on late-night TV, she manages to complete three goals at once: lampooning rival rocker Sinead O'Connor, offsiding Buttafuoco, defending the pope—and pulling off an astonishing hat trick of hypocrisy!

HYPO-CRITICAL GOAL #1: Defending the Pontiff—Madonna's photo-tearing comes weeks after Sinead O'Connor had ended her "SNL" appearance by ripping up a picture of the Pope and saying, "Fight the real enemy!" At the time of O'Connor's photo-tearing, the Sainted One publicly rapped the singer in an interview with RTE Irish state radio: "I think there's a better way to present her ideas rather than ripping up an image that means a lot to other people," Madonna said. "If she's against the Roman Catholic Church and she has a problem with them, I think she should talk about it." This statement came during the week when Madonna articulated her views on the Roman Catholic Church at a party promoting her book, *Sex*, where women dressed as nuns led crowds through a warehouse filled with leather-clad models engaging in simulated sex acts, and actors in priests' vestments "baptized" the crowd with chalices of champagne.

HYPO-CRITICAL GOAL #2: Offense to Buttafuoco—What Madonna meant to "articulate" by replacing the pope's image with that of Buttafuoco is a tough one. To vilify Joey Buttafuoco himself? Adulterous husbands? Men in general? Pedophiles? Regardless of her intent, Madonna taking a stand against Long Island's alleged Humbert Humbert seems kind of ironic coming days before the world would see her kiddie porn photo series in *Vanity Fair* that featured the 34-year-old feminist icon topless in pigtails and straddling a blow-up whale with her bottom exposed.

HYPO-CRITICAL GOAL #3: Hipcheck to O'Connor—Apart from all the political points Madonna scored on "SNL," the slap at O'Connor might also have aimed to sting the 25-year-old single mother and abortion rights activist, with whom Madonna had exchanged verbal blows before. A year earlier, O'Connor took the trophied Boy Toy to task for her faux feminism in an interview in *Spin* magazine, where she recalled that Madonna "said I looked like I had a run-in with a lawnmower and that I was about as sexy as a Venetian blind. Now, there's a woman that America looks up to as being a campaigner for women, slagging off another woman for not being sexy."

August 1993

Madonna takes her "first turn as journalist" in an interview in *Mademoiselle* magazine with Rosie O'Donnell, her gal pal and former castmate from *A League of Their Own*. Foregoing obvious lines of questions about her friend's three forthcoming movies, the cub reporter uses her first chance on the other side of the news desk to ask such probing questions as:

"If you were going out on a date with someone for the first time, would you rather have bad breath or a pimple on your nose?"

"Do you pick your nose when people aren't looking?"

and . . .

"Have you ever farted and blamed it on someone else?"

It probably won't get her a Pulitzer, but Madonna did shrewdly angle the story to cover the most pressing material, asking O'Donnell in no uncertain terms:

"Why do you like me better than all your other friends?"

and . . .

"What did you like best about working with me? Did I ask that question already?"

The Girlie Show World Tour concludes its New York run at Madison Square Garden. The show begins with a topless dancer shimmying down a pole and continues in a relentless burlesque of dancers simulating sex acts, all orchestrated by Madonna, who is alternately featured as circus ring master and Pierrot clown. Vendors hawk red roses in the aisles, setting the mood for a romantic surprise Madonna has planned between acts.

At the close of the "Holiday" number, performed in military costume, Madonna turns to her troop of dancers and calls one "sergeant" forward for rebuke. It seems that there are rumors afoot that he has had intimate relations with another member of the company and "knocked her up." Madonna only accepts answers in military fashion: "Yes, sir, Mrs. Sir. Yes, sir!" When the dancer says he plans to marry the company member, Madonna metes out punishment. She commands the "sergeant" to propose on bent knee and sing "You Are the Sunshine of My Life" to his fiancée. Madonna abruptly ends the ballad interlude because she claims it's making her sick, but before dismissing the couple, Madonna has them get down for twenty-five push-ups. When she asks the audience if they found the surprise romantic, Madonna has to prod them before they respond to her liking: "Yes, sir, Mrs. Sir! Yes, sir!"

The romantic display concludes with Madonna's rhetorical mutter about "ruining a good thing."

Fans are not moved to toss their roses on the stage.

A Super-Trivial Quiz—Part I

1. What is Madonna's favorite candy, and why?
   a. Mary Janes, because they remind her of the shoes that when well-shined would let boys look up her dress.
   b. $100,000 Bars, just because.
   c. Blow-Pops, because they're hard on the outside and soft in the middle. You can suck them or crunch them. And there's always a surprise inside.

2. What inspires Madonna to follow a strict vegetarian lifestyle?
   a. Compassion for animal rights.
   b. Concern for the bad karma she would accrue, just in case she were to be reincarnated as a cow.
   c. Belief that "vegetarians are paler."

3. "GROI!" is a clever acronym Madonna coined to better express herself during video edits with her musical colleagues. What does GROI stand for?
   a. Good going, Really Original, Inspired!
   b. Golly, Roll Over Iggy [Pop]!
   c. Get Rid Of It!

4. What did it cost Madonna to get her body in shape for her 1986 world tour?
   a. $39.99 for a pair of Pro-Ked sneakers and a couple of cheap jog bras.
   b. Nothing. Those nice Merchant Marines wouldn't take any money.
   c. $35,000 for personal trainer Rob Parr.

5. Which Biblical woman did Madonna name herself after when she was confirmed, and why?
   a. Mary Magdalene, because she had great tattoos.
   b. Medusa, because of her wicked hairstyle.
   c. Veronica, because she wiped the face of Jesus.

The correct answer to all questions is "c."

3 America's Most Unwanted

Deconstruction of a Wannabe

Meet Miss Wannabe, one of the girls who wants to be Madonna. She's just a silly girl, out for a good time, but has found herself in a jam. Her closet is spilling over with ten years' worth of Madonna hair fads and fashion accessories, and she can't decide which Madonna to be today. Should she wear her black mask? Or should she wear her bows? Poor little Miss Wannabe has too much to choose from. You can help her get out of the house by mixing and matching from any of the Madonna period ensembles collected in her wardrobe. You can put her underwear on first and then you can put it on last. You can play all day! But every time you dress Miss Wannabe up, don't forget to dress her down—for being stupid enough to want to look like Madonna.

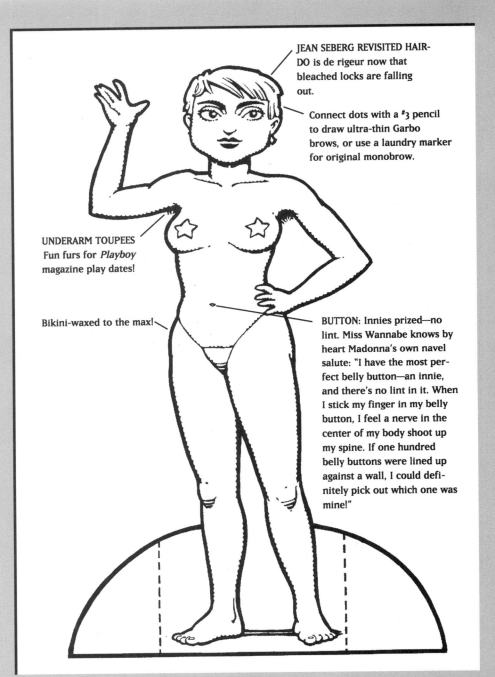

JEAN SEBERG REVISITED HAIR-DO is de rigeur now that bleached locks are falling out.

Connect dots with a #3 pencil to draw ultra-thin Garbo brows, or use a laundry marker for original monobrow.

UNDERARM TOUPEES Fun furs for *Playboy* magazine play dates!

Bikini-waxed to the max!

BUTTON: Innies prized—no lint. Miss Wannabe knows by heart Madonna's own navel salute: "I have the most perfect belly button—an innie, and there's no lint in it. When I stick my finger in my belly button, I feel a nerve in the center of my body shoot up my spine. If one hundred belly buttons were lined up against a wall, I could definitely pick out which one was mine!"

"I HAVE NIGHTMARES OF JEANNIE" hairpiece, signature top knot of Madonna's *Blonde Ambition* tour.

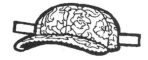

paste-on-mole

BASEBALL-STYLE HAT in floral print worn with brim flipped up for jogging, pulled down to hide from paparazzi. Miss Wannabe, who, like Madonna, disdains America's favorite pastime, never wears real baseball caps (Madonna is NOT a team player), and only attends spectator sports begrudgingly, when dating a player, donning black leather motorcycle cap.

DARK GLASSES work for day and for night (movie screenings, dance clubs, indoor basketball games) to dim flashbulbs — even if they are only make-believe!

CRUCIFIX EARRINGS
Pierced, of course.

DUMBBELL
Miss Wannabe's
signature clutch.

Cut off here!

CUT-OFF MESH T-SHIRT

Cut off here!

Cut a little here, too.

BLACK MERRY WIDOW Miss Wannabe titters whenever she wears her Merry Widow, keeping in mind *Playboy* magazine's words that Madonna's outre underwear is "not a celebration of Frederick's of Hollywood mentality but a parody of it, a distortion of the trappings of feminine sensuality."

GAULTIER HEAT-SEEKING MISSILE BRA
Goes where the action is!

LIKE RELIGIOUS ICON PENDANTS
Wear one or wear them all, because when it comes to worship, Miss Wannabe, like Madonna, is devoted to only one idol. You guessed it.

BOY TOY BELT BUCKLE
"Ironic" cinch—it doesn't mean what you think!

DIGITLESS GLOVES
The better for Miss Wannabe to claw her way to the top!

RECYCLED RUBBER BRACELETS
Miss Wannabe wears these typewriter O-Rings by the dozen and is armed for any adventure.

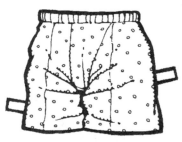

TROPHY SHORTS Spoils of preppy boy-toy conquest are worn victoriously with "Like a Virgin" white garter belt.

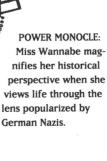

POWER MONOCLE: Miss Wannabe magnifies her historical perspective when she views life through the lens popularized by German Nazis.

DISCARDED RUNNING SHOES Miss Wannabe's most coveted possession are the sneakers Madonna once sweated in. Bought at an auction for $4,500—a bargain at twice the price!

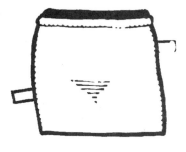

SARAN WRAP MINI
Miss Wannabe always feels fresh when she wears her skirt that clings like Saran Wrap. It looks small but it stretches.

BOWLER
Black, worn with white wedding dress.

DREADED TUTU Last removed from mothballs in '87 for *Who's That Girl?* look. Torn in fist-fight with Cyndi Lauper fans who claim it was theirs first.

tear here

tear here

GOIN' FISHIN' NET STOCKINGS
When Miss Wannabe wears these with her cut-off jean shorts, she never knows what she'll catch!

HEIDI FROM HELL
Miss Wannabe braids her hair in neat coils, picks up her stuffed toy lamb, and, wearing her sourest milkmaid expression, is ready to go to a *Sex* party!

49

4 Justify My Love Life

Cut them out! Collect them! Trade them with your fellow anti-fans! Here is your introductory set of Madonna Lover Trading Cards. Each fun, fact-filled card features sexual statistics, gratuitous anecdotes, and no-longer-personal information about a different Madonna lover: those she has slept with, teased or toyed with. Playmates include boyfriends, girlfriends, one-night stands, threesomes or moresomes, fiancés, and one heavy-hitting husband. Plus, you get two BONUS SPECIAL ISSUE cards: "Tackiest Moments of a White-Trash Hollywood Wedding" and "Sex With Madonna—Rules to Love By."

Once you start collecting Madonna Lover Trading Cards, you won't be able to stop—you can't possibly catch up with her! According to Madonna's first manager, Camille Barbone, the *Sex* maniac had already racked up a hundred men before her first hit record! "She plowed through boyfriends like party snacks," cheered *People* magazine.

Who makes the cut on Madonna's team? Well, first there are the ones she cares for: "Very rarely in my life have I had sex with someone that I didn't have real feelings of love for," she told *Vanity Fair*. Then there are the ones she doesn't: "I don't like most of the men I sleep with," she confided in *Truth or Dare*. Which statement is true? Who cares?! It just makes for more trading cards!

But you can't tell the players without these Score Cards. So start collecting today and look for future sets as they become available—supplies are unlimited!

TOMMY

YEARS PLAYED 1968

POSITION 10-year-old child in the wrong place at the wrong time.

HOME FIELD St. Andrew's Catholic School playground and convent.

THE PITCH One day on playground, Madonna ripped off her blazer and blouse and chased hapless boy around, topless. A nun grabbed her and explained that little girls did not take off their clothes and chase boys.

FIRST BASE The next day, Tommy gave Madonna her first kiss, in the convent. She later described the experience as "incredible!" There are no reports of his reaction, though there is story of boy named Tommy who suddenly went deaf, dumb, and blind at around the same time.

SAINT TOMMY Kiss changed Madonna forever, she said later. Until then, she had intended to become a nun, because they were "very sexy." Pope is still breathing sigh of relief.

RUSSELL "Cadillac Man" LONG

YEARS PLAYED 1973
POSITION 17-year-old, only man for whom "Like a Virgin" was true.
HOME FIELD Parents' house (first time); backseat of powder-blue '66 Cadillac. Car, dubbed by classmates "the passion wagon," was Madonna's favorite spot. She often drew her initials in steam on windows.
FIRST CAREER HOME RUN After movie, burgers, and Cokes, Long wondered how to maneuver 14-year-old Madonna home. She ended speculation by abruptly suggesting they go to his house. "I was so nervous I couldn't get her bra strap undone," Long recalled later. Madonna undid it for him. Then she egged him on by asking, "Do you want to do it or not?"
POSTGAME INTERVIEW "I considered it a career move," Madonna said later.

MICK JAGGER

YEARS PLAYED 1978
POSITION Lead singer of Rolling Stones, genuine musical talent.
PLAYING FIELD Plaza Hotel lobby.
ROOKIE SEASON According to Christopher Anderson, unauthorized scorekeeper of both Madonna and Jagger, the new Stones groupie joined regulars hanging around Jagger's favorite hotel. She had dark hair and chewed gum constantly. "This girl was obnoxious, but also very friendly," recalled veteran groupie named Kevin. "She'd walk up to you and say in a loud voice, 'I want to be a singer. I can sing anything. Wanna hear?' and then before you could tell her to shut up, she'd start singing and everybody would turn and stare."
NO RELIEF "There was no way to get away from this girl. She was there a lot, and she called herself a Jagger groupie . . . . I got the feeling she thought he'd help her with her career."
MAJOR LEAGUE BIMBO Several times, Jagger invited her upstairs. "They slept together back then," recalled Kevin. "She was wild and that appealed to him."

STEVE "Full-Tilt" NEWMAN

YEARS PLAYED 1983
POSITION Editor of underground rock monthly, *Island* magazine.
FIRST PITCH "We danced and she flirted outrageously," said Newman, who met Madonna at one of Keith Haring's parties. "Afterward, I sat on one arm of this big chair, and she sat on the other. Then she crooked her finger at me, leaned over, and gave me this deep, deep kiss. Right then I fell head over heels."
SIGNING BONUS *Island* magazine was Madonna's first magazine cover.
INJURY WORRIES Concerned about Madonna's reputation, Newman told Madonna he was afraid of being wounded and wanted a "full-tilt" relationship or nothing. She agreed to a committed relationship.
WARNING TRACK Newman discovered he was not the only man in Madonna's life when her fiancé, Jellybean Benitez, stormed into his bedroom one morning and dragged her out.
YER OUT! According to Newman, Madonna sat him down one day and said: "Here you are, just this chump publishing a little magazine on the Lower East Side that's never going anywhere. I'm making $200,000 this year, and I'll make ten times as much next year. It's just never going to work."

MICK JAGGER

DAN GILROY

YEARS PLAYED 1978–79
POSITION Guitarist/songwriter and music coach who opened bed and band to then Vagrant Voguer.
THE WIND-UP Gilroy met Madonna at a party. Found her "depressing."
THE PITCH Madonna went to her fastball: "Aren't you going to kiss me?"
OUT OF LEFT FIELD Madonna gave Gilroy poem she had written that was somehow autobiographical and also concerned Chinese tradition of foot-binding.
OFF-SEASON Madonna spent spring training of 1979 in Paris, where she was coached to be French singles hitter in Edith Piaf mold.
YER OUT! Back in American League, Madonna played drums with Gilroy's band, Breakfast Club, on Lower East Side circuit. When she demanded more at-bats with the microphone, teammates gave her the thumb.
POST-GAME INTERVIEW "It was like a roller coaster," said Gilroy after being sent to showers. "You go on for a few thrills, then it's over."
BIGGEST ERROR Strapping guitar to Madonna and teaching her her first chords.

DAN GILROY

MARK KAMINS

MARK KAMINS

YEARS PLAYED 1981–82
POSITION Mixmaster with nightclub rep as King of New Wave dee-jays.
FORMER TEAMMATES Kamins had worked on an album with David Byrne and signed U2 as freelance scout for Island Records.
HOME FIELD Second floor of Danceteria.
THE PITCH "I was flirting with him," Madonna recounted later.
SINGLE A four-track copy of "Everybody," which she persuaded him to play.
CONTRACT NEGOTIATION Kamins and Madonna agreed that if he could get her record deal, she would let him produce her first album.
CONTRACT RENEGOTIATION He did, she didn't.
POSTGAME RECAP He sued; they settled out of court.

ERICA BELL

ERICA BELL

YEARS PLAYED 1982–?
POSITION Sidekick, dancer, model, NYU grad student, owner of downtown Manhattan nightclub called Lucky Strike.
HOME FIELD Lucky Strike. Feeling sorry for starving Madonna, Bell hired her to tend bar. The gig lasted only two nights because Madonna "wanted to focus all her energy on her career, which she talked about incessantly."
FIRST BASE "I was intrigued with Madonna before she kissed me. But I can tell you one thing: once Madonna kisses you, you stay kissed."
COLOR COMMENTARY "How close were we? Well, we slept in the same bed," said Bell.
SPITBALLS "We stood on the curb and spit and spit and spit—until she felt satisfied that she could spit like a tough New Yorker. People were horrified, but we thought it was hysterical."
NIGHT GAMES "Madonna would say, `Rica, I am the best-looking white girl here, you are the best-looking black girl here, so let's do it.' Then we'd push people off the dance floor and take over."
BREAKING BALLS "We'd pick out the cute boys," Bell tells, "go right up and without saying a word kiss them on the mouth. Then we'd take their phone numbers, walk away, and while the guy was still watching, crumple up the number and throw it away."

JOHN "Jellybean" BENITEZ

YEARS PLAYED 1983–85
POSITION Mixmaster extraordinaire and influential producer.
HOME FIELD Funhouse discotheque, where Benitez was designated disc jockey.
THE PITCH "She had heard about him," singer Johnny Dynell has said, "she knew he could help her. So one night she walked right up to the deejay booth, grabbed him, and kissed him."
BRUSH BACK "She didn't bowl me over at first," Benitez said later.
SWINGING FOR THE FENCES "We both started to move at the same pace," recalled Benitez, who used his first paycheck to hire a personal publicist. "We're both very career oriented, very goal oriented. We both wanted to be stars." Others have described the relationship as a collision of two titanic egos.
YER OUT! After sharing a loft in SoHo and almost marrying him, Madonna called in rocker Prince as a pinch hitter after scouting him at the American Music Awards—where Benitez was her date.
OUT OF LEFT FIELD "He's a Scorpio and we both want to be stars, so it's tough going all the way," Madonna explained after affair with Jellybean was called on account of Purple Rain.

JOHN "Jellybean" BENITEZ

PRINCE

PRINCE (THE MIDGET)

YEARS PLAYED 1985

POSITION Musician, songwriter, genuine musical talent.

VITAL STATISTICS 5'3", 120 pounds.

ON DECK Like Madonna, Prince worships Marilyn Monroe. His Minneapolis house is filled with posters of tragic movie star.

THE WIND-UP First met backstage at American Music Awards, January 1985.

THE PITCH Prince called Madonna next day for date, to attend his upcoming concert at L.A. Forum.

UNSPORTSMANLIKE CONDUCT After having sex in back of his limo en route to a concert, Prince pulled out her panties onstage and rubbed them on his face, sniffing and making sexual gestures.

DOUBLEHEADER While Prince squired Madonna around Los Angeles, Madonna pursued her "serious relationship" with Sean Penn.

INJURIES Sean Penn's pride, wall. In jealous rage over reports of her affair with Prince, Penn punched hole in wall of Madonna's apartment. Soon after, Prince came over with plaster and helped Madonna repair it.

NICKNAME Midget. "Time to go visit the midget," Madonna said before date with Prince.

SEAN PENN (The Boyfriend)

SEAN PENN (THE BOYFRIEND)

YEARS 1985

POSITION Brattiest of Brat Pack, entree to Hollywood.

PREVIOUS TEAMS Penn had been engaged to Pam Springsteen (Bruce's sister) and actress Elizabeth McGovern.

VITAL STATISTICS 5'6" with wolf's head tattooed on forearm. Later had "Daisy"—a nickname for Madonna—tattooed on his toe.

THE WIND-UP On January 10, 1985, Madonna was filming "Material Girl" video and noticed "the guy in the leather jacket and sunglasses kind of standing in the corner, looking at me."

THE PITCH Madonna promptly threw Penn an icy glare, then shouted, "Get out! GET OUT!" Then presented him with a rose.

PLAYING FIELD Romantic dates to Marilyn Monroe's grave.

NICKNAMES His, Buddy; Hers, Pal.

RHUBARB At Manhattan restaurant, when Penn's ex-flame Elizabeth McGovern stopped by table to say hello, Madonna exploded into tirade of expletives and stormed out.

THE DIAMOND On June 16, Madonna was jumping up and down on bed, naked, in Nashville hotel, then stopped. "Whatever you're thinking," she told Penn, "I'll say yes to." He proposed, then two went to 7-Eleven and celebrated with jawbreakers.

OUT OF LEFT FIELD Madonna explained attraction this way: "I feel like he is my brother or something. In fact, when I squint my eyes, he almost looks like my father when he was young."

TACKIEST MOMENTS OF A WHITE TRASH HOLLY-WOOD WEDDING

1. Shocking-pink wedding invitation in style of Grant Wood's American Gothic, featuring Penn holding beer and Madonna wearing "ironic" Sean Toy belt and holding pitchfork.

2. Wedding is held at $6 million Malibu home of real-estate developer and friend Kurt Unger, according to British journalist Maggie Hall, "as a promotional setup for Unger, because his house was up for sale. Unger was hoping that by staging the wedding there, it would be enough free advertising to sell the house." It wasn't.

3. Steve Rubell vomits on dress of Debi M., Madonna's makeup artist, in limo en route to wedding (too many Quaaludes).

4. Madonna's 73-year-old grandmother trudges alone up mansion driveway and runs gauntlet of press.

5. Groom scrawls "Fuck off" in sand to helicopters passing overhead.

6. Paula Ciccone, Madonna's younger sister and maid of honor, cries while applying lipstick in the bathroom, and then flies into a rage: "I can't believe this is happening. This should be my wedding day, not hers. I should be the famous one. This career should be mine. All this attention should be mine."

7. Groom crouches in shrubbery by swimming pool waiting for helicopters to pass overhead, then fires at them with .45-caliber automatic pistol.

8. Bride wears black bowler hat as she marches down aisle to music from *Chariots of Fire*.

9. Ceremony lasts five minutes.

10. Newlyweds cut wedding cake, serve it to guests with their hands, and throw icing and cream at each other.

11. Penn stalks photographer milling through crowd and throws two punches, which are blocked, before having lensman ejected.

12. Penn dives under Madonna's skirts and comes out with red garter belt between his teeth.

SEAN PENN
(ROOKIE HUSBAND)

YEARS 1985–87

SULTAN OF SWAT On April 12, 1986, at neighborhood hangout Helena's, old friend David Wolinksi kissed Madonna hello on cheek and Penn savagely beat him. Wolinski pressed charges; Penn received $1,000 fine and one-year probation.

BAZOOKA JOE Madonna made new husband lock his guns away in strongbox. But Penn spent hours sitting on windowsill, swigging beer and randomly firing shots into backyard pool.

SLUGGING PERCENTAGE UP AGAIN Penn broke probation by punching extra on set of *Colors*. While Penn served 33 days of a 60-day jail sentence, Madonna was filming *Slammer*, later renamed *Who's That Girl?*

STEE-RIKE ONE! Penn's obsession with Madonna's extramarital affairs careened out of control. One day, he threw chair through window and smashed tureen of soup on floor.

STEE-RIKE BACK! Madonna hurled vase at husband's head and pummeled him.

STEE-RIKE TWO! Penn stuck wife's head in gas oven.

STEE-RIKE THREE! Pal tossed Buddy fully clothed into pool, twice, and repeatedly threatened to seriously harm her—although he later insisted, "I got most of the beatings."

SEAN PENN (Rookie Husband)

SEAN PENN (THE HUSBAND)
THE FINAL INNINGS

YEARS 1987–89

YER OUT! After disappearing for 4 days, Penn popped up at N.Y. apartment on Thanksgiving Day, expecting turkey dinner with trimmings. She served him with divorce papers instead.

EXTRA INNINGS Two weeks later, Madonna called off divorce.

A LEAGUE OF HER OWN Madonna stopped playing model wife. Appearing on "Late Night with David Letterman," she started rumors of lesbian affair with Sandra Bernhard. Next, stories report an affair with JFK Jr. Then she was seen in company of Warren Beatty talking about "working together" on *Dick Tracy*.

THE THIN LADY SINGS Madonna files divorce papers on January 5, 1989. She drops assault charges January 10.

MEMORABLE QUOTES, HERS "I don't believe in divorce, because I was raised a strict Catholic."

MEMORABLE QUOTES, HIS "You can continue to suck the big dick of Hollywood if you want to, but you can count me out!"

POSTGAME COMMENTARY Penn has not been arrested or in a fight since divorce, and has relationship with actress Robin Wright. After their daughter, Dylan, was born, Madonna sent enough nursery gifts to unnerve Wright, and a note of congratulations to Penn: "Silly boy, if you'd given me a baby, we'd still be together."

SEAN PENN (The Husband)

NICK KAMEN

YEARS PLAYED 1986–87

POSITON Singer/model with physical talent to make husband Sean Penn jealous.

SCOUTING REPORT Madonna first spotted Kamen on a jeans commercial, where he stripped to his underpants before a dozen gaping women in a laundromat.

SIGNING BONUS Madonna called aspiring singer at office of his record company and offered to write him a song. "There was something in his eyes that inspired me to write for him," she said. Then she called back and offered to produce it.

HOME FIELD L.A. studio where the two holed up for five days writing what would become Kamen's first single, "Every Time You Break My Heart"—a song ex-lover Steve Bray also helped write and produce.

INJURY (RECURRING) Sean Penn's pride, sprained and twisted. Determined to hold on to his position, Penn followed his wife onstage at an Amnesty International concert, picked her up, and carried her off.

NICK KAMEN

JOHN F. KENNEDY, JR.

YEARS PLAYED 1987
POSITION JFK's bachelor son, ticket to fantasy camp where
Madonna could act out Marilyn Monroe's second coming.
THE WIND UP Madonna confided to friends that, as undisputed
heiress to MM legacy, she felt fated to tag Kennedy Jr.
HOME GAMES To keep press from stealing their signs--since
Madonna was still married——they attended plays and parties sepa-
rately but ran home together. Other bases included health club
they shared in Manhattan; Central Park reservoir, where they
jogged; and Kennedy family compound in Hyannis Port.
STRIKEOUT According to family friends, Jackie O. scouted Madonna
as "a crass social climber, a tramp," and sacrilegious.
PERSONALLY AUTOGRAPHED SOUVENIR Funeral wreath with white
roses inscribed "My deepest sympathy" and card signed "M"—sent
after ex-hubbie Sean Penn dissed JFK Jr. at Tribeca party for having pitched woo to his ex-wife.
INJURIES Penn's pride, torn irreparably.

JOHN F. KENNEDY, JR.

SANDRA BERNHARD

SANDRA BERNHARD

YEARS PLAYED 1988—92
POSITION Comedienne, sexual provocateur.
WIND-UP In her stand-up routine, Bernhard begs Madonna to "be
my friend, come live with me, Madonna. Push me over the borderline, Madonna. Fuck up my head, Madonna."
FIELD OF DREAMS Madonna dreamed that she and Bernhard had
survived a catastrophe and were last two people on Earth. Then,
Madonna was sitting in audience when Bernhard described apoca-
lyptic fantasy in which she and Madonna survive World War III—
"but Sean doesn't." Sensing kismet, Madonna raced backstage to
meet her soulmate.
INJURIES Sean Penn's pride, sprained and twisted (again). At L.A.
opening of his play HurlyBurly, Madonna showed up late, accompa-
nied by Bernhard. At party later, Penn hissed at his wife, "You
cunt, how could you do this to me?"
POSTGAME WRAP-UP "It got out of hand and then I didn't want
to do it anymore," said Madonna after she dumped Bernhard.
LAST LICKS Bernhard seems to have revised her opinion of her
soulmate. At screening of Body of Evidence, Bernhard was admon-
ished for talking too loudly and shouted in response, "This is not
a serious film." She walked out before the movie was over.

WARREN "Old Man" BEATTY

WARREN "Old Man" BEATTY

YEARS PLAYED 1988—90
POSITION Longtime Hollywood star, director of *Dick Tracy.*
AGE 52, earning him Madonna's nickname of "Old Man."
FORMER TEAMMATES Joan Collins, Natalie Wood, Leslie Caron, Michelle Phillips, Julie Christie, Diane Keaton, Carly Simon, etc. etc.
PEP TALK "Sometimes I think, he's been with the world's most beautiful, glamorous women. I go, 'Oh my God!'" said Madonna. "Then there's the side of me that says, 'I'm better than all of them!'"
THE PITCH Madonna first went to Beatty to land role in *Dick Tracy.* "I saw the A list and I was on the Z list," she said later. But she was willing to do what Kim Bassinger, Kathleen Turner, and others weren't—work for union scale, $1,440 a week.
STEE-RIKE ONE! "Don't TOUCH me!" Madonna shrieked at Beatty, storming off set when he tried to put consoling arm around her.
STEE-RIKE TWO!! "Don't hide back there, Warren," Madonna commanded Beatty in *Truth or Dare.* "Get over here. You stink. You pussy man. . . . Are you going to be nicer to me now, Warren?"
STEE-RIKE THREE! Madonna wanted to include intimate messages Beatty left on her answering machine in *Truth or Dare.* Against his wishes, she tried to keep personal material in, suggesting they edit out Warren's voice and use subtitles. (Material was finally deleted.)

TONY WARD

YEARS PLAYED 1990, 1991—
POSITION Model, boy toy of summer.
VITAL STATISTICS 5'7", 170 pounds.
ON DECK One of mermen in Madonna's "Cherish" video. Had previously posed in *In Touch for Men.*
THE PITCH At her 32nd birthday party Madonna's brother Mario pointed out handsome, shirtless 27-year-old. Madonna walked over, put cigarette out on his back, and took him home as party favor.
SWITCH-HITTER Madonna dressed Ward in stockings, bra, panties, high heels, dangling jewelry, and made him up with lipstick, eye shadow, face powder. After adding beauty spot to make him look like her, Madonna paraded around with her new "girlfriend." Sometimes they went to parties where Madonna would sit in Ward's lap and tell him to be mute. She ordered him to shave off his mustache, which he did.
CHEAP SEATS Ward appears in "Justify My Love" video as lover tied up and fondled by a dominatrix as he is forced to watch Madonna make love with another man.
POSTGAME COMMENTARY, Madonna's: "He was a complement, but I insist that whoever complements me has his own identity."
EXTRA INNINGS Months after breakup, they were running bases together again.

TONY WARD

CHARLES BARKLEY

CHARLES BARKLEY

CHARLES BARKLEY

YEARS PLAYED 1993

POSITION Power forward, Phoenix Suns

SUNSHINE FAN Madonna, who admitted she knew nothing about basketball, called Barkley after he had been named League MVP and team was in playoffs.

BULGING OUT OF UNIFORM At Knicks-Bulls game, Madonna in too-small Adidas warm-up jacket scouts stands behind non-regulation sunglasses—indoors, at night.

GAME CALLED Barkley, estranged from wife Maureen, hotly denied having affair. "No, I have not danced with Madonna, I have not slept with Madonna," Barkley barked at reporters. "She's a very nice person. Very friendly. We met and had a fun evening. I haven't seen her again. There's no romance there."

TWO ERRORS Barkley admitted Madonna "called me in the middle of the night" before the Suns' semifinals victory. According to Madonna pal Anthony Keidis, lead singer of Red Hot Chili Peppers, "Barkley's been leaving [nasty] messages on my machine. [Barkley] showed up at my house at five in the morning and he was screaming. Ask him." Madonna's spokeswoman denied romantic triangle rumors.

COLOR COMMENTARY Madonna threatened to score next with Shaquille O'Neil. "I have jungle fever," Madonna reportedly told a friend.

BIG DADDY KANE

BIG DADDY KANE

YEARS PLAYED 1992—

POSITION Rap artist, genuine musical talent, Madonna's pictorial lover.

THE WIND-UP "I didn't want to be in the book," BDK told *Source* magazine.

THE PITCH A telephone call: "Ayyyo, Madonna's doing this book and she wants you in it. I think it'll be a good move, because you're not the only rapper in the book, but you're the only black man in the book." "Yeah, all right, cool," BDK said, taking the offer.

TWEENER BDK Poses out of uniform in paisley bikini briefs for photos with nude Madonna and model Naomi Campbell, also nude, in Oreo cookie fashion with Madonna sandwiched in middle.

TRIPLE PLAY BDK Playing with Madonna's genitals as she French-kisses Campbell, and in turn is played by Madonna as she fondles BDK's nipples.

LOCKER ROOM CONFIDENTIAL Answering Williams's charges, Kane told *Source*, "If stickin' my finger up in $60 million worth of pussy is going out, I will go out every mothafuckin' day. Plain and simple. I'm waiting for this here phone to ring and say, 'Yo, we got $70 million worth of pussy to stick your finger in this time.'"

INGRID CASARES

INGRID CASARES

YEARS PLAYED 1992–93
POSITION Jogging partner, gal pal M.V.P.
THE WIND-UP Introduced to Madonna by Sandra Bernhard.
NICKNAME Hers for Madonna, "M."
SWING, SWING, SWING In non-regulation boys-of-summer uniform, Ingrid wore three-piece suit to beach to French-kiss M for photos for *Sex*. Switch-hitting from real life to fiction, Ingrid becomes legendary player as star of M's sexcapades featured in same book. Odes to "imaginary" Ingrid include fantasy birthday party: "Just to show Ingrid how much I love her I let her French-kiss me and smear my lipstick," writes M in *Sex*.
SQUEEZE PLAY In final innings of party hosted by M for k. d. lang, Ingrid sees M headed for dugout and makes last-ditch effort to keep game alive. Legs splayed, she caresses M's rump and gives her good double-fisted squeeze. M reads signs and kisses Ingrid on lips, twice, then tousles Ingrid's hair before hitting showers.
BENCHED? When rumors fly that M has subbed Ingrid with new recruit, Jenny Shumizu, Ingrid balks to *Daily News*: "Me and M are still very much together. Hello!"
INJURIES Sandra Bernhard's feelings. After being dropped from M-team, Bernhard on Howard Stern radio show lamented being given the thumb: "There is such a thing as loyalty."

SPECIAL FANTASY ISSUE

CAUGHT WITH MADONNA: RULES TO LOVE BY

If you're ever caught in a tryst with Madonna—and this could happen to anyone—here are some guidelines to follow. Try to get it right the first time—so you don't have to do it again.

1. NO PDA (Private Display of Affection): Hand-holding, hugging, tender embraces are only appropriate on camera or at large parties.
2. FAKE IT: Simulated sex is the preferred act, because the lighting is so much better.
3. BEND YOUR GENDER: The more androgynous the better—go to the head of the party.
4. BOY TOYS WANTED: Males over 18 and IQs over 80—get off the bed! Take a number and wait in line!
5. BUY HER BOOK, *SEX*: It may not do much for you, but she'll want to see the receipt.
6. NO SPANKING: Forget what you heard in her songs and on Arsenio. "I say I want to be spanked, but it's like 'Try it and I'll knock your fucking head off.' It's a joke."
7. APPLAUD: The ideal foreplay. What orgasm is as satisfying as an ovation?

And still counting . . .

5

PriMadonna

THE BACKSTAGE RIDE!

ADMIT ONE

Congratulations!

☞ **YOU** have won a pass to PriMadonna Land —the Backstage Ride.

☞ **You've** seen some outrageous stuff in her overblown concert tours and videos, but in your worst nightmares you never imagined how HAIRY, how *Twisted,* how *Totally Out of Control* are the horror shows she puts on behind the scenes!

☞ **SEE** Madonna look on and giggle as her gorilla-boy bodyguards beat the living daylights out of the paparazzi. **WATCH IN AMAZEMENT** as the Star from Hell throws tantrums that leave the well-meaning assistant in tears. **LISTEN IN HORROR** as the Ultimate Bitch on Wheels terrorizes admiring fans to their faces and complains about them behind their backs, "like really overweight girls or guys with lots of acne that follow me around and pester me. It's frightening because not only are they bothering me, but they're horrible to look at, too." *FREAK OUT* as Pop Culture's Frankenstein provokes a frenzy of fear to feed her insatiable ego. And, finally, **WONDER** if this woman's 15 minutes will ever be up?

Read on...if you DARE!

THE BAD SEED

One of Madonna's earliest childhood memories is of sitting in the
driveway of her house when a
young neighbor girl came waddling
up in diapers. She looked up at
Madonna and handed her a dande-
lion. Madonna pushed her down. She later recalled that she was
mad because she was being punished at the time and that her first
instinct was to hurt someone who was weaker. "I saw in her innocent eyes the chance to get back at some authority."

She added that she was also enraged at the dandelion because
it is a weed that grows out of control on lawns and she only likes
things that are cultivated—a fine aesthetic distinction for someone
under five years old.

THE POODLES' CURSE

After Camille Barbone rescued Madonna from the streets, she took
her young protégée to Planned Parenthood, held her hand when her
wisdom teeth were removed, and on her birthday took her out to
Far Rockaway to see the ocean for the first time and treat her to her
first taste of lobster.

Later, Barbone asked Madonna to do her a favor
and pet-sit for her two poodles,
Norman and Mona. When Barbone
returned after her trip, she found
that one of her dogs had been
spray-painted orange and the other
pink. The helpless poodles had also
been graffitied with the words *Sex*
and *Fuck*.

"I was bored," Madonna told
Barbone. "I had to do something."

THE EGO HAS LANDED

"She acted every bit the star even then—even though she was nothing," said *Village Voice* columnist Michael Musto, who was part of another downtown group when Madonna was playing in her first band, Emmy. "She tested her microphone from every angle. She wouldn't let us have a mike check at all. And after we did our opening act, she wouldn't let us share the dressing room with her. Her manager would say, 'You have to leave. Madonna's getting dressed.' Even though that was the only dressing room for all of us. We insisted on staying anyway. I thought, 'This girl is not going anywhere. She's a major bitch. She's going to offend so many people and she's going nowhere fast.'"

BEACH BLANKET TERROR!

It was the height of Fashion Week in Paris in 1984 and Madonna's first single, "Holiday," was shooting up the less-competitive European charts. Italian designer Elio Fiorucci flew Madonna and her entourage to Paris to entertain at a party filled with fashion luminaries.

PriMadonna wasted no time in registering complaints about everything in sight. "She hated her hotel," said a Warner Brothers employee, "and she didn't like the chauffeur-driven car we provided her with. She didn't like the French press, so she refused to give interviews. In short, she was on a huge star trip way before she was a huge star and alienated everybody she came into contact with."

Asked to perform a song on a French version of "Saturday Night Live," a show called "Sex Machine," Madonna arrived at the beachfront location of the taping and immediately griped, "I don't want to dance in the mud."

"But it's not mud," the show's producer replied. "It's wet sand."

"I say it's mud!" she shot back. Then one of the letters from her Boy Toy belt fell into the sand. "She exploded," recalled the producer. "She made the Warner public relations woman, the driver, and two dancers look for the missing letter. 'Find the letter,' she screamed, 'or I'm not doing this fucking thing.'"

"She had people on their knees," the producer said later. "We were scrambling in the sand looking for the missing letter for half an hour." His summation of her behavior is blunt: "Madonna was vile! She behaved very badly. I suppose if she did that kind of thing now, people would find her brilliant. At the time, everybody said, 'Why are we putting up with this?' She was nobody then."

INVASION OF THE HARD-BODY

"She was 'The Material Bitch,' and that's how people would refer to her," said John McCormick, who worked at the Sports Connection, a prestigious Hollywood health club where Madonna worked out in the summer of 1985.

"She used to take aerobics with us and she used to stand in the middle of the aerobics room, with her arms straight out, and spin, and that was her space, and no one was to enter that....and pity anyone who was near her."

MISS THING LANDS IN L.A.

Even before the release of *Desperately Seeking Susan*, those around Madonna noticed that her personality had taken a turn for the worse. One night, personal assistant Melinda Cooper received a late-

night call from her boss, who had just arrived in Los Angeles. "I had arranged for a limousine to pick Madonna up at the airport," recalls Cooper, "but there was some sort of mix-up and it wasn't there when she arrived in L.A. She screamed profanities at me, calling me a cunt and all sorts of other terrible things. It was the first time she made me cry."

PHANTOM OF THE GREEN ROOM

The Live Aid Concert was held six months after the all-star recording session for "We Are the World," where producer Quincy Jones had instructed the superstars donating their time to "Check your egos at the door." The performers at the "Live Aid" benefit adopted the same selfless attitude—except Madonna. "The only one who acted like a superstar was Madonna," reported *USA Today*, which dubbed her a "prima donna." More than a dozen bodyguards and Sean Penn bulldozed her path, holding their hands up to block photographers there to record the event. Then Madonna switched dressing rooms. Twice. She finally installed herself in a room with the Beach Boys, Ashford & Simpson, and Eric Clapton.

The Disco Diva posed for only one photograph, for the cover of *People.* When she hurried through the green room on her way to the stage, her bodyguards instructed the stage personnel and technical crew not to look at her as she walked by. While onstage, her opening line was "I ain't taking shit off today!" Since no one expected any of the performers to use obscenities, there was no way the word could be bleeped off of the live broadcast.

HOMECOMING QUEEN FROM HELL

After the Madison Square Garden concert that closed her "Virgin" tour, a Homecoming Party was held for Madonna at New York's Palladium. Five thousand fans assembled to salute their heroine, two of her favorite go-go bands were flown up from Washington, D.C., and the whole space was lavishly decorated in Madonna-style lace and white roses. The guest of honor was, apparently, unimpressed. She finally breezed in through a side door at around midnight and rushed through the VIP room to a VVVIP area, where she was surrounded

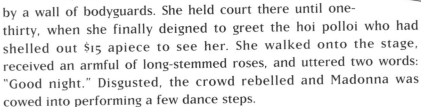

by a wall of bodyguards. She held court there until one-thirty, when she finally deigned to greet the hoi polloi who had shelled out $15 apiece to see her. She walked onto the stage, received an armful of long-stemmed roses, and uttered two words: "Good night." Disgusted, the crowd rebelled and Madonna was cowed into performing a few dance steps.

"I loved her," said Erica Yager, a disillusioned receptionist from New Jersey, "but now I like her less."

STING OF THE WASP WOMAN

At a cocktail party at Yoko Ono's at the Dakota, Madonna wandered into the kitchen, where David Bowie and Bob Dylan were talking. The Disco Belle soon rambled out into the living room, where the crowd was drinking cocktails, and blurted out:

"Thank God there's somebody here to talk to—there are only old folks in the kitchen."

THE M-BOMB

One night in Manhattan in the spring of 1992, Madonna was reported to have braved a bomb scare at the Roxy nightclub, staying to dance the evening away despite the apparent danger. But it was later reported that the bomb scare had been faked to give the Dance Floor Diva more room. A staffer circulated through the VIP room announcing to people, "You have to leave. There's been a bomb threat." Among those rushed out were Liza Minnelli, Sally Kirkland, and Kathy Najimy. Roxy manager Jason McCarthy later denied anything was said about bombs, though he admitted that Madonna was in the back of the club in the Bordello Room, when party organizer Kelly Cutrone asked to have the Crystal Room emptied so Madonna could spread out. McCarthy explained himself with a haunting phrase, "We were just following orders."

CHILDREN OF THE DAMNED

At Madonna's request in 1986, the Ciccone sisters and brothers were invited to a photo shoot for *Life* magazine. "It's an act of love," Madonna said. "They have always seen me in front of the camera. Now it's their turn."

During the session, a *Life* reporter asks Madonna et al. how her success has affected the family. Madonna was glib. "They ask to borrow more money," she said bluntly. "I don't think it's hurt them in the outside world. We are all very competitive. I think it's only natural."

The rest of the clan, however, had a different view. "It's difficult to walk in that shadow," said her brother Anthony, who was studying to be an actor in New York. "They pretend to be interested in you, but they really aren't." For Martin, a deejay in Detroit, his sister's fame was "a real pain in the ass."

After the Norman Rockwell–inspired shoot, the Ciccone brothers and sisters continued the Madonna-ordained family get-together at a nearby restaurant in Little Italy. Except Madonna, that is, who had other plans and a stretch limousine waiting. Dragging her Norma Kamali fake leopard coat, she left for a ride uptown with her bodyguard, her publicist, and her personal assistant. Her real loved ones?

IT FOLLOWED HER FROM THE TOILET!

One evening at Columbus, an Upper West Side trattoria and celebrity hangout, a Madonna fan was having dinner with her husband when she spotted the Star of Stars supping with her then-husband, Sean Penn. When Madonna went to the ladies' room, the fan saw her chance to make contact, and excused herself to the bathroom too. Big mistake.

After apologizing to Madonna for disturbing her, the woman gushed with compliments and flattery. Madonna iced her without a word of response, leaving the awkward fan to retreat to her table, where she finished her meal with her husband. Madonna may not have given her admirer the time of day, but Penn did have a few moments to spare and made sure to stop at the lady's table, where he cursed her out with a shockingly foul tirade that left fellow diners with jaws agape. Except Madonna, of course, who coolly stood by, tight-lipped as ever.

THE FURY

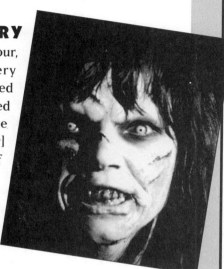

At rehearsals for the "Who's That Girl" tour, Madonna's head would spin over every technical glitch, wrong note, and botched dance step. "Madonna whined and sulked and blew up a lot," one roadie said. "She would swear a blue streak at [director] Patrick Leonard and push dancers out of her way if they goofed up. She'd pace up and down and throw tantrums—literally stamp her foot like some spoiled little girl if everything wasn't exactly the way she wanted. Everybody was afraid of her."

TEN TOES OF THE DRAGON LADY

While filming *Who's That Girl?*, a rip-off of Katharine Hepburn's classic *Bringing Up Baby*, Griffin Dunne expressed amazement that Madonna would insist that her first take was the best one and refused to repeat a scene.

In post-production, during the looping sessions in which actors are required to overdub unclear lines, the Artiste refused to cooperate, insisting that her first takes were the best. She relented only after her director, imploring her to overdub a single line of dialogue, literally knelt down and kissed her feet.

DON'T GO IN THE ELEVATOR ALONE!

When Madonna and Sean Penn attended the Mike Tyson-Michael Spinks heavyweight fight in Atlantic City, aides to Donald Trump reported to the New York *Post*'s Page Six that Madonna was incensed when a "civilian" (non-celeb) was allowed to ride in the same elevator with them. Aides said she insulted Trump and even made a nasty speculation "about his ancestry." They added that Madonna had called at the last minute asking for two tick-

ets to the fight, plus a round-trip flight on the Trump helicopter. "Donald went out of his way to rearrange things and get two seats for her," a spokesperson said. "Then she wanted two more for her bodyguards. Plus, we were told the tickets had to be for Mr. and Mrs. Sean Penn—'otherwise, he'll get upset.'" Another furious Trump staffer said: "I think she's a bitch. I have to tell you. We did everything but turn ourselves inside out."

AUGUST THE 16th—Part XXX

Devoted fans who marked Madonna's thirtieth birthday by buying tickets to see *Speed-the-Plow* were turned away at the door on orders from the star herself. "They said Madonna didn't want any disturbance on this night," said a 14-year-old girl who came in all the way from White Plains. "I don't understand. I'd never hurt Madonna."

Fans who came with gifts of roses received the same diffident treatment. Fifteen minutes before show time, the birthday girl threw the bouquets out her dressing room window.

NIGHTMARE ON 64th STREET

"Madonna beat me up," reported Keith Sorrentino, a 10-year-old fan from Staten Island, whose parents sued the superstar after she allegedly choked their son. Little Keith and his older sister Darlene were devoted fans. They knew when Madonna got up, where she took morning coffee, where she jogged.

They knew the name of her private secretary, when she left the theater (after performing in *Speed-the-Plow*) and from which door. What they didn't know was how Madonna felt about their adulation.

"We're her fans," Keith said innocently. "We were following Madonna out of the San Remo [co-op]. I ran in front and took her picture and she said, 'Please, not today, it's my day off.' We kept following her up different blocks . . . and that's when she started cursing me out—she's got some mouth on her—and threw me against the wall. Look. I got bruises," he told New York *Post* columnist Amy Pagnozzi, exposing a skinny arm.

Keith suffers from "regular nightmares," according to his attorney, who filed a $600,000 damage suit over the encounter.

Madonna denied the assault and the case was finally settled out of court.

> "That's right, I'm a fucking bitch," Madonna shouted at the screen in a theater showing the paparazzi documentary *Blast 'Em*, in response to an on-screen photographer who had called her "a fucking bitch."

STAIRWAY TO HELL

In July of 1992, Madonna asked the New York Society for Ethical Culture to stop giving shelter to fans and photographers who wait for her outside her Central Park West building. Most of the faithful are groupies who merely want an autograph, but Madonna requested that the philosophical league, which is headquartered across the street, kick them off of their steps. As one report put it, "Some think it's hypocritical of the almost virgin to be belligerent toward her followers after she's worked so hard to cultivate them. Not always the most gracious of idols, she's been known to tell the worshipful to 'Get a life!'"

THE MONSTER WHO CAME TO DINNER

When *Vogue* magazine hosted an exclusive dinner party in Paris for Madonna, the Lady of Honor decided she didn't want to wade through the aisles crowded with her guests—so she walked across an elegant tabletop in her spike heels and Gaultier gown.

THE SHINING

Madonna occasionally likes to remind the world that she's really just a girl from Michigan who hasn't lost touch with her working-class roots. "I've been known to wash a dish or two," she has said.

Cleanliness is, after all, close to godliness. But Her Holiness is not often close to the scullery staff. The High-Handed One would rather give orders to her personal assistants to leave notes on the chrome taps in the bathroom that read: "You have not polished enough."

THE HOUSE
ON THE HILL

"It was beautiful before. Now it's just disgusting," said Christa Spieth. "It makes you physically ill to look at it because it's the color of blood. . . ."

Spieth is but one of Madonna's neighbors who have been seeing red ever since she turned her $5 million landmark Castillo del Lago estate into what Hollywoodland residents now call Barnum & Bailey's. Five months after she moved into the thirty-two-room mansion once owned by Bugsy Siegel, Madonna painted the pristine white exterior platelet red, and for added umbrage accented it with fifteen-inch-wide canary-yellow stripes.

"It's her house. It's a free country," said publicist Liz Rosenberg, defending her client's latest outlet of artistic expression. True enough, there are no zoning laws that protect house color, but Crosby Doe, a preservationist who lives three doors down from the unsightly site, sees the house—every day—as a desecration. Ruing the day Madonna replaced the antique tiled roof, jackhammered out the tile in the center courtyard, and increased the property's shlock value by adding small concrete ornaments to the walls along the driveway, Doe asked in vain: "Does one have the right to take the crown jewel of the neighborhood and make a farce out of it?"

A Super-Trivial Quiz—Part 2

6. In a fax to writer David Handelman of the lyrics to a song called "Goodbye to Innocence," Madonna made a telling spelling error. Which word is the Hype Priestess not that familiar with?
    a. Sado-Masochism
    b. Sex
    c. Anonymity

7. Who is Madonna's personal hero?
    a. Mussolini
    b. Madonna
    c. Mother Teresa

8. What does Madonna claim to be her "favorite, favorite, favorite" music to listen to?
    a. Madonna
    b. Supertramp
    c. Baroque

9. What was Madonna's own prescription to treat depression?
    a. To down a pint of Häagen-Dazs and a Prozac chaser.
    b. To streak her hair, then streak down Hollywood Blvd.
    c. "Not to make [herself] feel better but to flagellate [herself] in other ways."

10. Complete the following Madonna quote explaining the artistic rationale for her preference of inexpensive sound equipment:
    "I use cheap microphones so it sounds dirty and raw—like...
    a. the *Deep Throat* soundtrack."
    b. Sammy Hagar."
    c. the bottoms of my feet!"

The correct answer to all questions is "c."

7

The Pantheon of Madonna Busters

Like a Lamentation

Behold, the heroes assembled in the Pantheon
The Righteous Few who have witnessed the cursed tide
    of Madonnaism
That has swept across our shores
    And showed the courage to stand tall against it.

Here are the noble men, women, and children
    Who covet not platinum or solid gold,
    Who would not go on bent knee to worship at the video altar
    The unholy images of the Fallen Star who tours on Earth.

Inscribed on these Tablets are the names of those
    Who have held their heads above
    the Deluge of Madonnamania.

Written in this book are the praiseworthy deeds
Of those who resisted the cult of the Self-Anointed One.

Let all who have rejoiced in the Parables of the Pantheon
Take from its pages a reverence for the unsung heroes among us
Who draw their purse strings and turn their dials
    Building a heavenly dam against Her boring "Rain"

Pat them on the back and say unto them "Hallelujah!"

ST. ANDREW'S CATHOLIC SCHOOL, NUNS OF

Fed up with young Madonna's antisocial misbehavior, the religious women washed her mouth out with soap and, when that failed, taped it closed. It was the last time anyone was able to shut her up. For good measure, Madonna later complained, "I got hit on the head with rulers by hostile nuns."

CAMILLUCCI, GREG

The manager of the Russian Tea Room hired Madonna for the job of checking coats at the 57th Street landmark, for $4.50 an hour. "She worked here for two months and was, well, an okay hatcheck girl," he recalls diplomatically. But he made up for his mistake by firing her unceremoniously when she repeatedly insisted on wearing the outfits fashion commentator Mr. Blackwell would later describe as "a nomination for a poverty-party centerpiece." "I fired her because, well, her costumes were outrageous," said Camillucci. "They just seemed out of place here."

COSTNER, KEVIN

"It was neat," he said in a brilliantly understated put-down of Madonna's overblown "Blonde Ambition" stage show. (The wittiest comeback Madonna could muster was a mock-puking gesture—finger down her throat—made, bravely, after Costner had already turned his back.)

HALL, ARSENIO

Appearing on Arsenio's show to plug her "Blonde Ambition" tour, Madonna made for an unwelcome guest, taunting Arsenio about "being dumped" by Paula Abdul and dissing the late-night host's hair. Arsenio kept his cool, but in a subsequent interview with *Ebony* magazine, he dressed her down: "First, Madonna, I will never have to work for you because I have as much money as you have. Number two, I've seen your dancers and ... I'm nothing like them. They work for you. I work with you. Point number three is that you wanted to be black when you were little, but you are not black, so don't try to understand blackness. It is not your place to dictate black hair care or fashion. You have borrowed our sound but not our sensibilities, so don't make an attempt to tell me how I should look."

HARRIS, NIKI

The back-up singer for Madonna refused Madonna's invitation to work on the "Like a Prayer" video. "Burning crosses," she explained, "meant something to me as a black woman."

ITALY

A big salute to the country that has done the most to oppose the Self-Anointed One despite—or because of—the fact that she is half-Italian.

Don Guiseppe Lepore: The local parish priest of Pacentro, Madonna's ancestral home, Lepore was first to speak out against a proposed shrine to the not-so-virginal Madonna at the town square. The statue was a thirteen-foot bronze representation of a scantily dressed Madonna singing into a microphone. A battered suitcase held together with string sits at her feet, symbolizing the twenty thousand emigrants who left Pacentro for America. Echoing the Vatican's condemnation of Madonna's thoughtless, random display of crucifixes and other religious symbols as sacrilegious, Lepore warned that any such statue would forever mark Pacentro as a modern-day Sodom.

Romans: On her "Blonde Ambition" tour, Madonna played to a small stadium with at least two thousand empty seats and was forced to cancel a second performance because of low ticket sales and a general strike threatened by labor unions. Scalpers sold tickets to the first show at cost or less. The state-run RAI television network dropped plans to record the concert for future broadcast.

Bambina De Giulo: Madonna's 82-year-old great-aunt decided against making the journey from Turin to Rome to see her famous family member. "Of course I'd like to see her and hug her—after all, it is an honor to have such a famous relation," she told a Rome newspaper. When pressed, however, Bambina revealed her true opinion: "What do you want from me? The girl is a singer, just a singer. In my times, we didn't behave like that!"

The Excelsior Hotel: The beautiful hotel in Florence, which overlooks the river Arno, turned Madonna away from their door though she was ready to pay for an entourage of fifty for a week. "We've had bad experiences with other pop singers whose reputations have been nowhere near as terrible as hers," sniffed a spokesman. "We won't have her here."

KADOKAWA, HARUKI

A low bow to the managing director of Kadokawa Publishing Company, who agreed to pay $1 million for the Japanese rights to publish *Sex*—but who canceled the lucrative deal when he was appalled by the photographs in the book.

LLOYD'S OF LONDON

Always on the lookout for another publicity stunt, Madonna got the idea of insuring her breasts after filming *Dick Tracy*. She set-

LLOYD'S
LLOYD'S OF LONDON

tled on the figure of $6 million—apiece. The insurance company disagreed with her self-assessment and turned her down.

O, JACKIE

After John F. Kennedy, Jr., took Madonna to visit his mother, Jackie hit the roof and warned her son to stay away from Madonna. According to a family friend, she felt Madonna would exploit the Kennedy name for publicity, and basically that she was a crass social climber, a tramp—and still married to Sean Penn.

SAN REMO, CO-OP BOARD OF

For refusing to sell her a $1.2 million apartment. The Material Girl was ready to spend a cool $100,000 per room for a twelve-room apartment in the fabled twin towers across from Central Park at West 74th Street. But the San Remo co-op board said "NO!" According to reports, Madonna was so anxious to share an elevator with such celebrity residents as Diane Keaton, Dustin Hoffman, Robert Stigwood, and Princess Yasmin Khan that she showed up for her co-op board interview in very un-Maddonaish threads—an unrevealing black dress accessorized with a demure string of pearls and only two large gold crucifixes. But the co-op board saw through Madonna's straitlaced look, possibly recalling less conservative images of the week before when pictures of Madonna in the buff were published in *Playboy* and *Penthouse* magazines.

LEACH, ROBIN

For standing up to Madonna's threats and creating the documentary *Madonna Exposed*, in which he invited all the little people in Madonna's life to give testimony on television to the injustices Madonna had committed against them. Leach claimed his inspiration for his show that meant to "lift the camouflage" came at the raunchy launch party for *Sex*.

"That party reminded me of pre-Nazi Germany. In came Madonna, dressed as Heidi. I kept thinking 'Somebody is playing a joke on us.'"

Trying to block *Madonna Exposed*, Madonna had her lawyers, her publicist, and manager Freddy DeMann phone and fax everyone who ever had anything to do with Madonna and forbid them to cooperate with Leach. Madonna even banned the showing of her ubiquitous music videos. But Leach prevailed and used his air time to poll millions of viewers with the rhetorical question "Has Madonna gone too far?"

SIBLINGS, CICCONE

"I was the tattle tale of the family. I was the rat fink," Madonna says, recalling her early years in a family of eight brothers and sisters. Perhaps in retaliation against their sister the snitch, perhaps just for sport, Madonna's siblings used to "torture" her, according to Madonna, who says a favorite trick of the Ciccone brothers and sisters was to get some clothespins and hang their biggest sister from the backyard clothesline by her underpants. "Or they'd pin me down on the ground and spit in my mouth."

BROWN, JULIE

Give it up for comedian Julie Brown, for making mincemeat of Madonna's bogus vanity project *Truth or Dare* with her excellent spoof, *Medusa—Dare to Be Truthful*. In the pseudo-rockumentary that also features Chris Elliot and Bobcat Goldthwait, Brown is fictional pop-diva Medusa, who embarks on her "Blonde Leading the Blonde" world tour and performs moving ballads: "Vague," "Expose Yourself," and "Like a Video," proving herself to be FAR COOLER than her real-life counterpart, Madonna.

EVANSVILLE, CITIZENS OF

After Madonna called their town "boring," the citizens of this

Chicago suburb struck back. While a helicopter carrying a national television crew hovered overhead, more than three hundred townspeople gathered in a parking lot to send her a message. Amid chants of "Madonna, get a life," they spelled out her name—inside a circle with a red line running through it.

KATZENBERG, JEFFREY

For dashing Madonna's hopes of starring in the film version of *Evita*. Heeding his own call for austerity, Katzenberg would not succumb to the perils of hypecasting even as Madonna was just emerging as box-office boffo for her autodocumentary, *Truth or Dare*. He refused to spend more than $25.7 million to bring *Evita* to the screen. That figure fell nearly $4 million short of what producer Robert Stigwood had budgeted for the film with Madonna as its star.

RIVERA, GERALDO

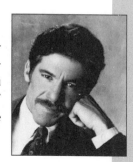

Around the time the *Truth or Dare* brouhaha was fizzling out, Madonna phoned in to the nationally televised talk show "Geraldo" and offered to appear on the program if host Geraldo Rivera would "make out" with journalist Kurt Loder on air. The two men were cheered for respectfully declining.

MAILER, NORMAN

For being "too busy" to interview Madonna for *Rolling Stone* magazine.

8 Feminist or Slut?

In a few moments you will take your final examinations for "Madonna 101—Feminist or Slut?"

Over the course of the last ten weeks we have studied the concept of Madonna as a feminist. We've learned that the theory rests on the argument that Madonna is a strong, sexually liberated woman in control of her medium and her message. Madonna is lauded for shocking the system and applauded for exercising her right to free speech—but what is she really saying?

We have heard opinions of theorists who would have you believe she is a musical version of such sexually

> "Madonna has a far profounder vision of sex than do the feminists. She sees both the animality and the artifice. Changing her costume style and hair color virtually every month, Madonna embodies the eternal values of beauty and pleasure. Feminism says 'no more masks.' Madonna says we are nothing but masks.... Through her enormous impact on young women around the world, Madonna is the future of feminism."
>
> --Camille Paglia, Op-Ed page, The New York Times

provocative thinkers as Germaine Greer, Margaret Sanger, or Dr. Ruth. We heard media pundit E. Ann Kaplan discuss the MP, or Madonna Phenomenon, in terms of Madonna's performance in the "Material Girl" video: "Madonna [is] the female star who perhaps more than any other embodies the new postmodern feminist heroine in her odd combination of seductiveness and a gutsy sort of independence."

Madonna herself has sounded confused on the subject, claiming, "I want to say to Gloria [Steinem] and the gang, 'Hey, lighten up. Get a sense of humor.'" On the other hand, she describes herself as a "very good role model," charging that "anyone who is upset with me is repressed."

Now it's time for you to come to your own conclusions. Complete this final exam by checking one of the two boxed choices at the end of each statement or anecdote drawn from Madonna's life and work.

Have a good summer!

1. "From the time that I was very young, I just knew that being a girl and being charming in a feminine sort of way could get me a lot of things, and I milked it for everything I could." —Madonna
   ❏ FEMINIST   ❏ SLUT

2. "She kept wearing scanty panties and the shortest miniskirts in [junior high school] to make the boys notice her," according to former classmate Colin McGregor. He and his friends begged her and the other cheerleaders to perform their cheers so the boys could see their panties. The girls, knowing full well what the boys

were after, refused—except Madonna, who cartwheeled for the boys alone.

❑ FEMINIST   ❑ SLUT

3. "Manipulating people, that's what I'm good at." —Madonna
   ❑ FEMINIST   ❑ SLUT

4. Madonna first became interested in performing through her junior high school ballet teacher. She has recalled that once when she wrapped a towel around her head, he told her that she had a face like an ancient Roman statue. "No one had ever talked to me like that before. I latched on to him like a leech and took everything I could from him." —Madonna
   ❑ FEMINIST   ❑ SLUT

5. "Oh, no. I thought of it as a career move." —Madonna, when asked if she mourned the loss of her virginity at fourteen
   ❑ FEMINIST   ❑ SLUT

6. "Madonna's big kick in high school was drinking," Colin McGregor remembered. "At all the parties she was always the one who fell off the chair 'drunk.' But the thing was she wasn't drunk at all." It seems Madonna pretended to be under the influence in order to make out with boys, and then the next day acted as if she didn't remember a thing.
   ❑ FEMINIST   ❑ SLUT

7. When Madonna's first manager, Camille Barbone, brought her 16-year-old cousin to catch Madonna's show,

Madonna ordered the teenager to "stand in front so I can see you." That way during the performance she could grab him by the collar and sing into the teenager's face. Later Barbone discovered the two making out in her dressing room, and Barbone wrenched the two apart. "He's awfully young," Barbone chided Madonna. "Yes," Madonna replied with a shrug, "but he's awfully cute."

❏ FEMINIST ❏ SLUT

8. "Madonna always had at least three guys going at a time," according to former lover Mark Kamins. "Each one of us was there to fulfill a separate need in her life....The cast of characters changed practically every week."

❏ FEMINIST ❏ SLUT

9. According to several sources, Madonna often cruised Manhattan's Lower East Side in her limo, picking up young Latino men and having her way with them. Madonna intimate Erica Bell has described these joy rides by saying, "You could go down to Avenue D and find dozens of guys who'll tell you they were picked up by Madonna. And they'd be telling the truth." Bell remembered riding with Madonna and "picking up two or three at a time." Sometimes she'd be satisfied with just a kiss, "but if she really liked the kid, she'd just rip off his clothes and do whatever she wanted with him while we drove around New York."

According to Mark Kamins, Madonna sometimes brought the destitute boys home to her luxurious apartment on the Upper West Side. "She ran a Puerto Rican stud farm up there," he said.

Wasn't there any risk the boys would tell someone about the experiences after she had abandoned them? "These were just banji boys, downtown kids," Johnny Dynell, a close-hand observer, has said. "Madonna was smart. She knew nobody would believe them."

❏ FEMINIST   ❏ SLUT

10. According to Erica Bell, Madonna's pick-up technique was always the same: "She tells them they are wonderful, flatters them, flirts with them—then sucks whatever it is she wants out of them."

❏ FEMINIST   ❏ SLUT

11. Between scenes in *Desperately Seeking Susan*, Bobby Martinez helped Madonna relieve the tensions of acting in her first feature film. "We did it in the trailer, man," Martinez has bragged, "with everybody standing around outside. They'd call her, she'd run out to do a scene. Then she'd come back and we'd do it again."

According to a worker on the set, it was no secret that there was plenty of free parking at Madonna's camper. "Her trailer would be rocking back and forth like there was an earthquake or something. Sometimes, you'd hear groaning inside. Afterward a guy would come out—sometimes two different guys in the same day. 'Like a Virgin' had just come out, so we all had a good laugh."

The only one left out, it seems, was fiancé Jellybean Benitez, who stormed in and out occasionally in jealous fits.

❏ FEMINIST   ❏ SLUT

12. "Warren insisted I get fatter. He wanted to pour me into my dresses. I gained ten pounds. So much depends on the look. It's so stylized. I had to bleach my hair again, pluck my eyebrows. It was traumatic to get the hair right. Hair is the most important

thing to Warren. He would walk around me like a vulture, making me feel like the ugliest thing in the world. And the dresses! We were at Western Costume, and he'd say, 'Tighter, tighter, cut it down lower.' I felt like a mannequin, a slab of beef. I was treated that way on the set—the lust factor." —Madonna, explaining what she agreed to do to play Breathless Mahoney in *Dick Tracy*

❏ FEMINIST   ❏ SLUT

13. Just as *Ladies' Home Journal* listed Madonna alongside First Lady Barbara Bush and Supreme Court Justice Sandra Day O'Connor as one of America's most powerful women, Madonna attended a Gaultier fashion show in order to catch a glimpse of her model boyfriend Tony Ward, who was in the show. As Ward paraded down the runway, Madonna picked up her dress to show him that she was not wearing underwear.

❏ FEMINIST   ❏ SLUT

14. During a performance of her concert tour in Paris, Madonna threw her panties to France's premier, who had a seat of honor in the audience.

❏ FEMINIST   ❏ SLUT

15. Playing her concert in Spain, Madonna set her sights on actor Antonio Banderas. She decided to make him fall in love with her—until Banderas's wife scared Madonna off with a murderous look. The singer resorted to griping that Banderas "probably has a really small penis."

❏ FEMINIST   ❏ SLUT

16. Lamenting the loss of husband Sean Penn in *Vanity Fair*, Madonna reminisced, "Sean was very protective of me. He was like my father in a way. He patroled what I wore. He'd say, 'You're not wearing that dress. You can see everything in that.' But at least he was paying attention to me. At least he had the balls. And I liked his public demonstrations of protecting me."
   ❏ FEMINIST   ❏ ANYTHING BUT

17. In *Truth or Dare*, Madonna confided to Sandra Bernhard that she doesn't like the men she sleeps with.
   ❏ FEMINIST   ❏ SLUT

18. Membership has its privileges at Club Nine, a Manhattan night spot where male members must have sexual equipment of nine inches or more. According to Jasmine Boyd, Madonna arrived at the West Fifties penthouse for a "specialty party," glammed up in a gold tinsel wig with a trio of bare-chested Latino men wearing slave collars in tow.

   "She called them her toy boys," Boyd said, going on to describe how one of the collared youths handed Madonna a tape measure as they all unzipped and she conducted a measuring contest.

   "She would measure each one with great ceremony and write down the results in a little black book," said Boyd. "Then she put a leash around the biggest guy—and I do not mean around his neck—and led him off to a bedroom."

   According to Boyd, Madonna boasted about her talent for divining a man's true genital worth by weighing his bulge with her gaze. Although, in an interview with *The Advocate*, Madonna denied that she cares about size, at least one former friend confirms that "it's no joke....She's not interested in somebody who's not...above average."
   ❏ FEMINIST   ❏ SLUT

19. "I'll flirt with anyone from garbagemen to grandmothers."
    —Madonna, on "The Tonight Show"
    ❏ FEMINIST   ❏ SLUT

20. "As Big Boy, Al Pacino was always smacking my butt and my face.
    I hated him, I loathed him. He'd tell me the dirtiest jokes, suck on
    his cigar like it was some sort of weird phallic symbol, and just be
    a pig....Every time I expressed my distaste for him, he'd smack me,
    which is also what happens in the movie. He made me cry some-
    times," Madonna recalled the work on the set of *Dick Tracy*.
    Plotting revenge against what she considered to be degrading sex-
    ist treatment, Madonna waited for the rehearsal of the big dance
    scene in which she, as Breathless Mahoney, suddenly dropped the
    fake fur coat she was wearing to the floor, revealing that she was
    naked. "He didn't know where to look," she recalled her victory
    later.
    ❏ FEMINIST   ❏ SLUT

21. By her former manager's account, Madonna had had "at least
    one hundred lovers" between her arrival in New York in 1978
    and her first hit record four years later.
    ❏ FEMINIST   ❏ SLUT

22. "Generally I don't think pornography degrades women. The
    women who are doing it want do it. No one is holding a gun to
    their head. I don't get that whole thing." —Madonna, in *Sex*
    ❏ FEMINIST   ❏ IDIOT

9 Where's That Girl?

Where's That Girl?" is a nearly impossible game of hide-and-seek that simulates the real world. The places and adventures you are about to encounter are drawn from actual Madonna hangouts and experiences. As in life, the object of the game is to do everything in your power to avoid contact with the Omnipresent One.

OBJECTIVE: To complete a trip around the world and return home again without having your vacation wrecked by intrusions of Madonna music, movies, headlines, magazine covers, or personal appearances.

PLAYING PIECES: You are represented by a choice of charms: Pepsi—which Madonna will never represent; Academy Award—which she'll

never win; Key to Bay City, Michigan—which she will never possess; Nike sneaker—which she wouldn't wear.

TO PLAY

Position all charms in your Living Room. First player rolls die and moves charm forward number of spaces indicated, then follows directions given in that space. Complete your American tour before advancing to next page and the trip abroad.

SANCTUARY SPACES

Soundproof room, Hospital, and Vatican. If you land in a Madonna Danger Zone three times in a row, or are otherwise instructed to seek Sanctuary, advance or move back to nearest Sanctuary space. Recuperate from your encounter with Madonna by spending your next turn playing a Truth or Dare Card.

FAT FAN SPACES

Land on any space marked by an obese wannabe boy or girl and you can transform a Madonna Danger Zone to a Safety Zone, since Madonna has a horror of fat people, and is above all repelled by her fat fans. "Fat is a big problem for me," says the Aerobicized Wonder. "It sets off something in my head that says 'overindulgent pig.'"

COMMEMORATIVE COIN

In the event of a tie, flip this coin. Heads, you've ended your trip around the world in the holy city of Jerusalem, where you can tour without fear. Rumors that Madonna is performing here are false, started by M herself when she announces to cheering crowds: "Israel, Israel, Israel. Finally, after all these years, I'm in your holy city!" When, in fact, the star of stars is not in Jerusalem, but geographically confused in Tel Aviv. Tails, on your way home you make a stopover in Puerto Rico, where Madonna is onstage rubbing the island's flag between her legs. You lose.

TRUTH: Can you sing two lines of "Material Girl"?

DARE: Sing them.

TRUTH: Have you ever seen *Shanghai Surprise*?

DARE: Pretend you're taking a Madonna Studies course at Harvard and it's time for your final project. Undress as far as you dare and streak through class. Get an A.

TRUTH: What would gross you out more: licking the back of a Madonna postage stamp from Grenada, or cleaning your bathroom floor with your tongue?

DARE: Pretend to call Madonna's psychiatrist up on the phone. Tell the shrink why she sucks.

TRUTH: Have you ever wondered if you're the one who's weird because you don't fantasize about kissing pierced nipples?

DARE: Find a picture of Madonna—you can use any one in this book—and pretend you have just been introduced. What would you say?

TRUTH: Have you ever had a dream or a nightmare involving Madonna?

DARE: Tell us about it.

TRUTH: If you had five minutes to go on a sweepstakes rampage of Madonna's closet, which clothing and accessories would you destroy first?

DARE: Name three actresses worse than Madonna.

TRUTH: Have you ever praised Madonna's singing, acting, or "ability to market herself"?

DARE: Pretend you're the head of Time Warner and Madonna's contract is up for renewal.

TRUTH: Do you own a Madonna album?

DARE: Go get it and use it as a Frisbee.

TRUTH: If you were in jail and had to share a cell with one of Madonna's movie characters, which one would you pick? Breathless Mahoney, the sex-crazed psycho-killer from *Dick Tracy*; Rebecca Carlson, the sex-crazed psycho-killer from *Body of Evidence*; or Bruna, the sex-crazed psycho-killer from *A Certain Sacrifice*?

DARE: Compose a letter of apology from Madonna to Marilyn Monroe.

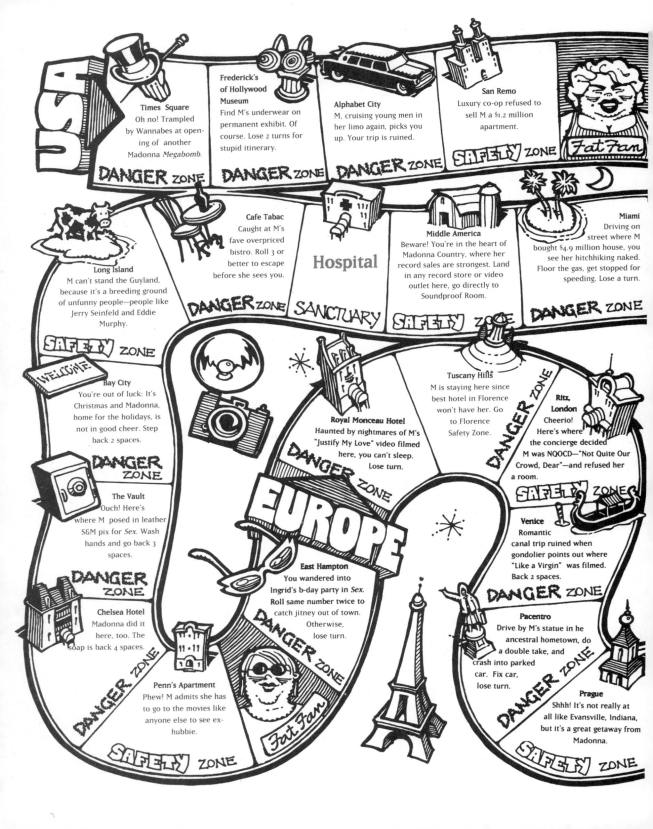

USA

Times Square
Oh no! Trampled by Wannabes at opening of another Madonna *Megabomb*.

DANGER ZONE

Frederick's of Hollywood Museum
Find M's underwear on permanent exhibit. Of course. Lose 2 turns for stupid itinerary.

DANGER ZONE

Alphabet City
M, cruising young men in her limo again, picks you up. Your trip is ruined.

DANGER ZONE

San Remo
Luxury co-op refused to sell M a $1.2 million apartment.

SAFETY ZONE

Fat Fan

Cafe Tabac
Caught at M's fave overpriced bistro. Roll 3 or better to escape before she sees you.

DANGER ZONE

Hospital

Middle America
Beware! You're in the heart of Madonna Country, where her record sales are strongest. Land in any record store or video outlet here, go directly to Soundproof Room.

SANCTUARY

SAFETY ZONE

Miami
Driving on street where M bought $4.9 million house, you see her hitchhiking naked. Floor the gas, get stopped for speeding. Lose a turn.

DANGER ZONE

Long Island
M can't stand the Guyland, because it's a breeding ground of unfunny people—people like Jerry Seinfeld and Eddie Murphy.

SAFETY ZONE

Bay City
You're out of luck: It's Christmas and Madonna, home for the holidays, is not in good cheer. Step back 2 spaces.

WELCOME

DANGER ZONE

The Vault
Ouch! Here's where M posed in leather S&M pix for *Sex*. Wash hands and go back 3 spaces.

DANGER ZONE

Chelsea Hotel
Madonna did it here, too. The soap is back 4 spaces.

DANGER ZONE

Penn's Apartment
Phew! M admits she has to go to the movies like anyone else to see ex-hubbie.

SAFETY ZONE

EUROPE

Royal Monceau Hotel
Haunted by nightmares of M's "Justify My Love" video filmed here, you can't sleep. Lose turn.

DANGER ZONE

East Hampton
You wandered into Ingrid's b-day party in *Sex*. Roll same number twice to catch jitney out of town. Otherwise, lose turn.

DANGER ZONE

Fat Fan

Tuscany Hills
M is staying here since best hotel in Florence won't have her. Go to Florence Safety Zone.

DANGER ZONE

Ritz, London
Cheerio! Here's where the concierge decided M was NQOCD—"Not Quite Our Crowd, Dear"—and refused her a room.

SAFETY ZONE

Venice
Romantic canal trip ruined when gondolier points out where "Like a Virgin" was filmed. Back 2 spaces.

DANGER ZONE

Pacentro
Drive by M's statue in he ancestral hometown, do a double take, and crash into parked car. Fix car, lose turn.

DANGER ZONE

Prague
Shhh! It's not really at all like Evansville, Indiana, but it's a great getaway from Madonna.

SAFETY ZONE

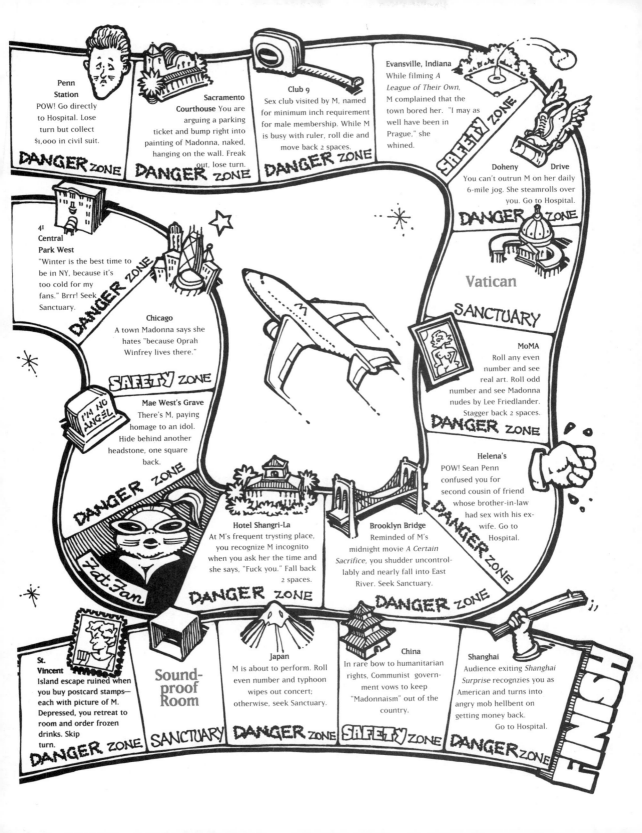

Penn Station POW! Go directly to Hospital. Lose turn but collect $1,000 in civil suit. DANGER ZONE

Sacramento Courthouse You are arguing a parking ticket and bump right into painting of Madonna, naked, hanging on the wall. Freak out, lose turn. DANGER ZONE

Club 9 Sex club visited by M, named for minimum inch requirement for male membership. While M is busy with ruler, roll die and move back 2 spaces. DANGER ZONE

Evansville, Indiana While filming *A League of Their Own*, M complained that the town bored her. "I may as well have been in Prague," she whined. SAFETY ZONE

Doheny Drive You can't outrun M on her daily 6-mile jog. She steamrolls over you. Go to Hospital. DANGER ZONE

Vatican SANCTUARY

41 Central Park West "Winter is the best time to be in NY, because it's too cold for my fans." Brrr! Seek Sanctuary. DANGER ZONE

Chicago A town Madonna says she hates "because Oprah Winfrey lives there." SAFETY ZONE

MoMA Roll any even number and see real art. Roll odd number and see Madonna nudes by Lee Friedlander. Stagger back 2 spaces. DANGER ZONE

Mae West's Grave There's M, paying homage to an idol. Hide behind another headstone, one square back.

I'M NO ANGEL

Helena's POW! Sean Penn confused you for second cousin of friend whose brother-in-law had sex with his ex-wife. Go to Hospital. DANGER ZONE

Hotel Shangri-La At M's frequent trysting place, you recognize M incognito when you ask her the time and she says, "Fuck you." Fall back 2 spaces. DANGER ZONE

Brooklyn Bridge Reminded of M's midnight movie *A Certain Sacrifice*, you shudder uncontrollably and nearly fall into East River. Seek Sanctuary. DANGER ZONE

Fat Fan

St. Vincent Island escape ruined when you buy postcard stamps—each with picture of M. Depressed, you retreat to room and order frozen drinks. Skip turn. DANGER ZONE

Soundproof Room SANCTUARY

Japan M is about to perform. Roll even number and typhoon wipes out concert; otherwise, seek Sanctuary. DANGER ZONE

China In rare bow to humanitarian rights, Communist government vows to keep "Madonnaism" out of the country. SAFETY ZONE

Shanghai Audience exiting *Shanghai Surprise* recognzies you as American and turns into angry mob hellbent on getting money back. Go to Hospital. DANGER ZONE

FINISH

10 The Immaculate Rejection

The Critics Look Back

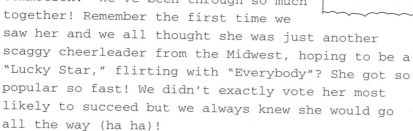

It's hard to believe a decade has already passed since the girl from Pontiac, Michigan, with big dreams and big hair first came into our lives. It seems like only yesterday that little Maddy Ciccone started "Causing a Commotion." We've been through so much together! Remember the first time we saw her and we all thought she was just another scaggy cheerleader from the Midwest, hoping to be a "Lucky Star," flirting with "Everybody"? She got so popular so fast! We didn't exactly vote her most likely to succeed but we always knew she would go all the way (ha ha)!

We've sure come a long way since the "Virgin" years. Remember how we laughed the first time she showed us her belly button?!

Maddy was always trying so hard to be popular.

She wanted to be tight with our crowd 'cause the Crits are the arbiters of cool. She'd do anything to get our attention. Who else would run her own underwear up the flagpole, and then parade around in public wearing the flag!

We ranked on her for being a "Material Girl," always asking "Where's the Party?" It was like, reality check! Do you know how to spell superficial? Who thought she would come into "Vogue"? That all along she'd been bottling up so much "Blonde Ambition"? And then "Truth or Dare" was a really excellent idea for a movie. As if! We couldn't believe it when someone actually wanted to publish her diary!

But through it all, the Crits were there. Even when Sean and the other crushes had come and gone, we came out to hear every new song, saw every show, and sat through every movie (arghhhh!). But then, that's what it means to be a Crit.

It's been ten years now and looking back we realized we could barely remember all the crazy things she said and did. So we put together this scrapbook filled with our favorite impressions and fondest memories of the girl we'll always "Cherish." NOT!

Love ya, Maddy! (HA!)

Forever,
the Crits

"This woman needs to see a good vocal coach before she attempts another tour. And one hopes that the next time she performs here, she will have learned not to toss tambourines into the air unless she's going to be able to catch them."
—Robert Palmer,
The New York Times

Memories of Radio City performance, 1985

Memories of "Material Girl," 1984

"'Material Girl'. . . may have sounded a bit like Carmen Miranda. What everybody noticed, however, was the video, in which Madonna shamelessly reinvented the wheel, lifting wholesale Marilyn's courtroom dance sequence from *Gentlemen Prefer Blondes* and flushing it of its satire. Subtlety, Madonna well knew, butters no parsnips in the pop marketplace. 'Material Girl' was crass, vulgar, obvious, charmless, and virtually definitive of the grasping zeitgeist of 1984. It was, naturally, her biggest hit to date, and probably remains so. . . .

"If truth be told, Madonna herself does not precisely exude sexuality. What she exudes is more like will, iron self-discipline, and, of course, punctuality, that courtesy of monarchs. In her 'Ciao, Italia' video, decked out in various gymnastic outfits and body-pumping to the screams of tens of thousands in a soccer stadium in Turin, Madonna looks perfectly able to make the trains run on time."
—Luc Sante, *The New Republic*

Memories of
"Borderline," 1983

"She understands how books work, if not how they develop. Effective books—as cast by Mozart or Holland-Dozier-Holland—proceed naturally from a melody's shape.

"Madonna's books are willfully imposed, unavoidable masses that enter a tune like Soviet tanks rolling into Prague. They stick all right, but then we could all sing 'Parsifal' start to finish if we'd heard it as often as 'Borderline.'"
—Steve Anderson, *The Village Voice*

"As in her other movies, Madonna shows no sign of how to act, walk, wear makeup, dress, or, for that matter, how to get gang raped properly. She doesn't even scream on key."
—*Hot Talk* magazine

Memories of
"A Certain Sacrifice," 1985

"Awesome in its awfulness."
—Roxanne T. Mueller, *Cleveland Plain Dealer*

Memories of
"Shanghai Surprise,"
1986

Madonna "acts and emotes with all the conviction of a guest in a sketch on a Bob Hope special."
—Douglas D. Armstrong, *Milwaukee Journal*

Memories of "Who's That Girl?", 1987

"The character Madonna played was nothing more than a phony cliche pop rebel, weirdly oblivious, dancing around in Pee-Wee Herman sweetie jerky hops, wreaking unfunny, gun-crazy havoc, and haggling in a Philly screech that sounds like a cross between Judy Holliday and Leo Gorcey. It's a movie in which the cougar has all the best lines."
—Michael Wilmington, *The Los Angeles Times*

"She moves as if she were operated by a remote control unit several cities away."
—Dennis Cunningham

Memories of "Speed-the-Plow," 1988

"Madonna was the weakest thing in it."
—David Richards,
The Washington Post

"No, she can't act."
—Howard Kissel,
New York *Daily News*

"She can afford to pay for a few acting lessons."
—John Simon,
New York magazine

Memories of "Like a Prayer," 1989

"If we don't love the new Madonna video, 'Like a Prayer,' we don't love ourselves. Think: She is literally the only pop star for whom doing a soft drink commercial represents nothing like a sellout....Her race issues are revealed for what they truly are. In ...the sequence [that] features Madonna writhing around in front of a field of burning crosses, a move which neatly reduces one of our nation's most potent symbols of evil into what amounts to flattering back-lighting."

—Jim Farber, New York *Daily News*

"The movie is about style, and that's why Madonna gets by. She's an element in the design.... She's an awful actress, but she's adequate as a masochistic, two-dimensional floozy."
—David Denby, *New York* magazine

Memories of "Dick Tracy," 1990

"When it comes to writing, she makes a good plumber."
—Vicki Goldberg, *The New York Times*

"Sex is the three-letter word Madonna chose for her just-released, long-hyped book. 'Ego' would have been better. Or perhaps 'Why'"?

—Marsha Kranes, New York *Post*

"Compared to [*Sex*], *Hustler* and *Screw* are far wittier, more irreverent, and, yes, more arty than this mess. (And a lot more economical.)"

—Andrea Peyser, New York *Post*

"This imagery, like most of Madonna's work, is secondhand, borrowed from the work of Robert Mapplethorpe (himself a master of photographic quotation), Calvin Klein's annoying Obsession ads, and self-important S&M movies like *The Night Porter*....One cringes to think what all the prepubescent Madonna wannabes will make of the book's relentless equation of sex and power, its sadomasochistic view on human relationships...."

—Michiko Kakutani,
The New York Times

"The soft-porn book of what Madonna wishes were her true sexual fantasies."
—*The Village Voice*

*Memories of "Body
of Evidence," 1992*

*Memories of
"Erotica," 1992*

"Spreading herself out on the floor or climbing atop a car in a parking lot and raising her skirt for [Willem] Dafoe, she's a coarse unmysterious object, a seeming escapee from 'The Robin Byrd Show.'"

—David Denby,
New York magazine

"If her libido were as weak as her concept of musical passion, who would ever get excited? This aural sex is mostly mediocre groove robbing."

—*People*

"To criticize Madonna for her narcissism is to complain that water is wet."

—Jim Hoberman

"Madonna's predominance is not the end of the world. Shit, the end of the world's gotta be more interesting."
— Steve Anderson,
The Village Voice

"This disco star of the '80s really isn't a very good singer. She's great if you like a singer who sounds like Little Bo Peep, but with her bleating vibrato, it sometimes makes her sound like a sheep in pain."
—Dennis Hunt, *Los Angeles Times*

"She is nakedly ambitious, manipulative, exploitive. Her facial expressions run the gamut from 'fuck you' to 'fuck me.' She has a reputation for having clawed her way up over the bodies of softer and weaker humans, most of them men. (In New York, when she was still rising to fame in the early eighties, some spoke of her as McDonna—over one billion served.) She is shallow, obvious and as vulgar as a belch.
—Michael Kelly, *Playboy*

"The trouble with selling yourself as a sex freak as distinct from a sex symbol is that it requires a new twist of the bizarre each time at bat. Marilyn Monroe is the most enduring of this century's sexy pinups. Whatever her private hells, she sparkled and shimmered on the screen, never transgressing propriety. Where Monroe was subtle, Madonna is coarse. Monroe enticed, Madonna bludgeons. Monroe was fun, Madonna embarrasses. Monroe winked a sexy innocence, Madonna is crude and lewd. With each new hustle, Madonna becomes more lurid, more blasphemous—and more pathetic. In her latest shock schlock, she confesses it would be 'neat' to have sex in a church."

—Ray Kerrison, New York *Post*

"Madonna offers something new under the sun: vicarious self-absorption. It takes a special kind of imagination to identify with a solipsist."

—Joseph Sobran, *National Review*

"If MTV hadn't come along when it did—knocking Andy Warhol's 'Everyone will be famous' dictum from 15 minutes down to three—Madonna might have been nothing more than a pop history asterisk."
—Richard Harrington,
The Washington Post

Is Madonna the Anti-Christ?

If Madonna accepts the possibility that she lives under the Devil's dominion, maybe we should prick up our ears. It sure would explain a lot: her penchant for rubbing crucifixes on her crotch and other wacked-out responses to Christian icons; her constantly changing identities; all the talk about ruling the world; all the boasts that she'd rather "walk through a fire than around it." If the bells aren't ringing yet, here are nine freaky facts that spin around one central frightening question: What if Madonna's inexplicable ascent to superstardom, in spite of her virtual lack of talent, was not just a coincidence of marketing genius and chutzpah?

Freaky Fact #1—David Koresh worshipped her.

The Branch Davidian cult figure who led his followers to their deaths in an inferno at their compound in Waco, Texas, David Koresh often spent the night playing his guitar, watching MTV, and fantasizing about Madonna, according to Kiki Jewell, one of Koresh's few surviving followers. "He thought Madonna was [put] in the world for him," she said.

Freaky Fact #2—Exited from Room #1313 in opening sequence of _Desperately Seeking Susan._

Freaky Fact #3—May have performed voodoo on Joey Buttafuoco.
Two days after Madonna tore up a picture of Buttafuoco and made an enigmatic command to "Fight the real enemy" on "Saturday Night Live," Buttafuoco was shot at. Buttafuoco, when asked on "Larry King Live" if the two events were related, said they might be, due to Madonna's star status.

Freaky Fact #4—Black Magic Concert Performance?
Launching her _Blonde Ambition_ tour in the Tokyo suburb of Chiba, on Friday the 13th under a full moon while storm clouds gathered and the heavens unleashed torrents of rain, Madonna staged a mock confession while suggestively dressed, straddling an altar, making suggestive gestures with an incense burner, and smashing a crucifix to the ground.

Freaky Fact #5—Controls her manager with "voodoo doll."
"When Madonna doesn't agree, she has a doll, and she squeezes it in all the right places, and I feel pain," Madonna's manager, Freddy DeMann, quipped to _Vanity Fair_ magazine.

Freaky Fact #6—Sings about a "Synagogue of Satan."
In "The Beast Within" version of her "Justify My Love" album, Madonna sings about a "Synagogue of Satan," a quotation from the Bible's Book of Revelations. The lyrics were formally protested by

the Simon Wiesenthal Center for having an anti-Semitic content, which Madonna later denied.

Freaky Fact #7—Admits affinity for dead things.
"Oh, everybody I like is dead," Madonna has said.

Freaky Fact #8—Would travel through cemeteries at night.
Seymour Stein, who signed Madonna to Sire Records in 1982 from his hospital bed, has said of her, "She's someone who would take a shortcut through a cemetery at night to get somewhere. You could tell in her eyes."

Freaky Fact #9—*Who's That Girl?*
The answer may lie in one of the film's stray lines of dialogue. In the movie, Griffin Dunne snatches his gold card away from Madonna, who has just used it to buy semi-automatic weapons, and demands: "Just tell me, I won't be upset, I just want to know. Are you the anti-Christ?"

"Be nice,
because everything you do
comes back to you.
I should know."
—Madonna